Because What You Do
Matters.

Bruce

Breaking Through Plateaus

How to Get Your Business Back On a Double-Digit Growth Curve by Creating a Culture That Automatically Produces It

Bruce D. Johnson. President
Wired To Grow

Celeritus Press

Breaking Through Plateaus: *How to Get Your Business Back on a Double-Digit Growth Curve By Creating a Culture That Automatically Produces It*

Copyright © 2012 by Bruce D. Johnson

ISBN-13: 978-0615614038

Printed in the USA by Celeritus Press

Dedication

To my one and only, my wife, Jacquie — who
still rocks my world, loves me unconditionally,
leaves me breathless, tolerates my unbelievably
long list of idiosyncrasies, and makes me want
to be a better man. After almost three decades
of marriage, I am still hopelessly, heels-over-
head in love with her!

Table of Contents

Introduction

If you've been stuck on a plateau for any length of time, my guess is that you've already tried a lot of different strategies and tactics to get your business (or organization) off the plateau you're on—and yet, despite all your best efforts, nothing seems to have worked.

You've brain dumped, you've brainstormed, you've read books, you've gone to conferences, you've bought programs, you've probably even tried coaching or consulting or a peer advisory group—and yet you and your business (or organization) are still stuck.

You've probably been told that the "secret" to getting your business back on a growth curve is to do something "simple" like raise your prices. Or add more upsells or cross sells. Or start using social media. Or upgrade your services. Or create a "blue ocean." Or develop more "raving fans." Or begin using pay-per-click advertising. Or systemize your referral process. Or …

And while all of the above are great ideas, they haven't worked for you. You've tried what has seemed to work for "everyone else" (after all, the testimonials you've read are killers), but none of the standard ideas/strategies/tactics/solutions seem to work for you.

If that sounds like you, then you're going to love this book. Why? Because for the past several years I've been wrestling with the following question, "Why is it that a strategy or tactic that seems to work so well for one business, doesn't work so well for another?"

My conclusion is that the discrepancy is caused by a series of drivers that reside behind the application of a strategy or tactic that accelerated growth companies possess, that plateaued companies simply don't.

In other words, there is a culture in growth companies (especially accelerated growth companies) that makes the implementation of a tactic or strategy more effective. On the other hand, if you take that same strategy or tactic and apply it to a plateaued company, because the right drivers aren't present in that company's culture, the strategy or tactic simply doesn't work (or doesn't work as effectively).

Now, while that statement may not feel like a very positive observation if you're leading a plateaued company, it really is. Why? Because the good news behind the drivers of growth companies is that they can be learned. Your company's culture can be changed. That means that, once you get a handle on what the growth drivers are, you can begin to adjust your company's culture to reflect that driver.

Then, once your company's culture is adjusted, you'll find that the very same strategies and tactics that you've tried to implement in the past that haven't worked — now will. Why? Because culture matters more than you think. It's not just the strategies and tactics themselves that matter; it's the culture that lies behind them that matters as well.

Which, of course, leads to one very important question, "So, what are the drivers that need to be a part of my company's culture?" I'm glad you asked. Because if you want to break through your company's current plateau and get back on a growth curve so that you can build a bigger, better, faster, and more profitable business (or organization) you're going to want to keep reading! The ten "secrets" that lie in the pages ahead can radically change everything for your company. Even better, the sooner you apply them, the sooner you'll be back on a growth curve (and wondering, "Why didn't I do this sooner?").

Also, as you begin reading this book, may I encourage you to read it in chunks — i.e. take one driver at a time and implement it. Plus, feel free to read this book in any order you desire. You don't have to start with Driver #1 and then move on to Driver #2, #3, #4, etc. Go ahead and scan the table of contents. Find where you think you have the greatest need and start there.

Finally, I designed this as an application-oriented book (why else take the time to read it). However, that also means that you could easily get overwhelmed if you tried to read it from cover to cover and apply everything all at once.

To avoid that feeling, may I encourage you to keep this book on your desk (or a nearby bookshelf) and return to it frequently because every one of the issues it addresses, is an issue you'll have to address over and over again for years on end.

So make friends with this book. Refer to it often. Apply the lessons within. And if you will, I'm confident that this book will become a trusted companion for you on the incredible journey in front of you!

To your accelerated success,

Bruce D. Johnson, President
Wired To Grow

P.S. Before you get started I want to remind you of one of life's irrefutable laws — which is, "What you put in, is what you get out!" Therefore, as you read through this book, I want to encourage you to not only read it — but to interact with it! Mark it up. Underline key phrases. Create your own notes. Star important ideas. Talk back to me (by writing in your margins) — especially if you disagree.

But mostly, make sure you do the application sections at the end of each chapter. After all, the value of a book is found, not in you completing the reading of it, but in what it changes in you and your world. Therefore, if you want to reap the most value possible from the ideas contained in this book, make sure you continually focus on this key question, "What can I apply from this _____ (chapter, paragraph, idea)?" If you do that consistently, this book will truly be both a business and life-changing experience for you!

Final Introductory Note: As you read through this book and encounter the ten drivers of accelerated growth, I want to encourage you to never let yourself think, "I know that." Why? Because whether or not you "know" something is irrelevant. The only relevant questions, whenever you're learning something are, "Am I doing that?" If not, "Should I be doing that?" And if you're doing that, "Am I maximizing that?" to which the answer is always, "No!" Why? Because no one maximizes anything. Everything can be improved.

"There are basically no companies that make good slow decisions. There are only companies that make good fast decisions."

Larry Page (Co-founder of Google)

Chapter 1
"Move Faster, Succeed Sooner."

Driver #1: Speed of Implementation

How fast are you and your team at implementing an idea? For example, when you finish a meeting and a decision has been made, how fast do you and your people execute that idea? Right away? Within a day? Within two? Within a week? Within a month? Or is it longer than that? If your business is plateaued, my guess is that you responded toward the longer side of those options — and that's a problem.

Now, while I'm not a huge fan of ordinals as in, "The number one thing you need to do is ..." when it comes to the question of, "What is the single, most important driver of fast growth companies?" I have to break my rule. This is number one. While the remaining nine drivers aren't in any specific order, this one is.

Speed of implementation is unquestionably the single greatest differentiator between slow and fast growth companies. In simplistic terms, it's the difference between, "Ready, Fire, Aim!" and, "Ready, Aim, Fire!"

Google could easily be the poster child for this principle. The past several years have proven that they have no problem at all with coming up with an idea, putting it out in the world — in imperfect form — and then tweaking it in response to the feedback they receive from their users/customers.

For example, when Apple came out with the iPhone, Google had no problem at all getting Android out quickly — even though it wasn't even remotely comparable to the iPhone. Google Chrome has undergone multiple revisions since its release. Google Catalog has been in development for years and often returns data from catalogs several years old. And Google Answers has never caught on.

Yet, Google still continues to be a highly profitable and fast growth company. Why? In part, because they've created a culture where it's okay to fail. Where it's okay to get something out fast and let the market determine whether it's a winner or a loser. Where it's okay to not hit 1.000 every time you're up to bat. And it is differences like this one that continues to drive the rapid growth of Google.

So, why is it then that more businesses, especially small and medium-sized businesses (SMBs) don't do this? Answer: because most SMBs have fallen victim to the slow growth disease of, "Analysis paralysis." Rather than acting fast, they tend to ponder, revisit, discuss, debate, and then postpone until they can, "work everything out."

I'm continually amazed at how long it takes many of my clients to implement ideas that they know could make a positive difference — that could help grow their business faster, allow them to lead it more effectively, create less stress in their lives and make them more money. Which raises an important question, " Why?" What is it that drives analysis paralysis?

In my work with owners and CEOs of SMBs, I've come to the conclusion that there are four main causes/issues that drive most organizational or personal tendencies towards analysis paralysis.

1. **Fear**

   For some people, the primary driver of analysis paralysis is their fear. It could be the fear of success or the fear of failure or the fear of rejection. But what stops them from taking action on what they "know" could help is a negative expectation about a future event. That's what fear is, isn't it?

   For example, if you believe that hiring a new sales rep could significantly add more revenue to your company but aren't willing to pull the trigger, you ought to ask why? If you're like a lot of business owners and CEOs it may be because you're thinking, "What if it doesn't work out?" "What if they don't produce?" "What if all I end up with is a huge expense and no additional revenue?" If you're thinking like that, what's holding you back is fear — fear of failure.

Note: This doesn't mean that you should go out and hire an additional sales rep. But it is a very real world illustration of what fear is. It's a "negative expectation about a future event." You (or I) could just have easily thought, "Boy, having an additional sales rep working full-time on generating more leads and converting more of them into sales will surely make my life easier — and make us a whole lot more money than just having me give a small portion of my time to marketing and sales." Either thought could be valid. However, one leads to action while the other doesn't.

While discussing fear may appear to be a "soft" issue, it does have a very "hard" impact on most businesses. In fact, I'm continually amazed at how large a role fear plays in most businesses — especially plateaued ones — and how it keeps them from doing the things they know they ought to be doing to grow.

2. **Personality**

There are certain personality types that are more action-oriented while others are more given to analysis paralysis. For example, in the Myers-Briggs typology, one of the four main categories of personality types is "SJ" (a type which accounts for 40% of the entire population). SJs, by nature, have an incredibly difficult time acting fast on something new because they want to do things right — which is the dominant driving force of an SJ.

On the positive side, SJs are great workers. When they have a system or know exactly what's expected of them, they'll follow through and make it happen better than most other types. But, on the negative side, they have a difficult time taking action when something isn't clearly spelled out or there's not sufficient proof that a course of action is the right course of action.

Now, this doesn't mean that an SJ can't overcome analysis paralysis. Typologies are descriptive, not prescriptive. An SJ can overcome his natural tendency, just like an introvert can overcome his tendency towards isolation and solitude and learn to network at large networking events. The change just needs to be done intentionally. Unfortunately, if someone has a tendency towards a certain behavior, in this case, analysis paralysis because of their nature, and they don't do something intentionally to overcome it, they'll never change — which, in this case, means never becoming a fast acting leader of a fast growth business.

3. **Beliefs**

The third reason why many leaders of SMBs have a tendency towards analysis paralysis is because they have a set of beliefs that anchor them there. For example, if you're one of those people who believes that something has to be perfect before it goes out, then you'll probably continually fall victim to analysis paralysis and you won't take action. Or if you believe that, "Doing something quickly is bad because when something is done quickly, mistakes are made," then you'll probably remain stuck in analysis paralysis. You won't execute fast.

Remember, all behavior is driven by beliefs. So if you or your business has a behavior that isn't working for you (in this case, not executing quickly), then you need to discover what the belief is behind that behavior — and then change it).

For example, if you discover that the reason you don't implement quickly is because you believe that something has to be perfect before it goes out the door, then you've got to change that belief — or your business will never be a fast growth business.

One of my favorite lines for those who struggle with perfectionistic tendencies comes from Tom Peters who so succinctly says,

"Do it right the first time is stupid." Tom Peters

No one does anything perfectly the first time. Perfection doesn't exist this side of heaven. It's unattainable. So let it go. Instead, pursue excellence, which is simply doing the best you can with what you have in the amount of time you have to do it. That is attainable!

4. **Structural issues**

    The final reason why a number of businesses and business leaders get stuck in analysis paralysis is because the systems they've set up in their businesses make it difficult for anyone to act quickly. For example, some organizations and businesses are set up with a committee structure where a committee has to approve a decision before action can be taken — which, by definition, hinders execution. Or others are set up with a checks and balances structure where multiple people have to sign off on a decision before it can be executed. Again, this hinders quick execution.

    But the one I find most frequently in small or medium-sized businesses is the one where the owner or CEO has become the bottleneck. In other words, too many entrepreneurial leaders struggle with letting other people in their organizations make decisions (especially big ones) without their approval. In essence, they end up creating structures where they, the point person, have to sign off before any significant action can be taken — which clearly hinders their business' ability to grow rapidly.

    What's interesting about these kinds of leaders is that they're often proud of the fact that their companies don't have lots of "structure," or "committees," but in fact they do — it's just a structure or committee of one! What they often don't see is that they've become the bottleneck who's hindering their people from taking action (and therefore, their business from growing).

Now, while plateaued and slow growth businesses are marked by analysis paralysis, fast growth companies are marked by the opposite. And four of the main contributors that help them create a fast growth culture are as follows.

1. **Few layers of bureaucracy**

    Few things hinder fast execution more than having to go through various approval channels. At the same time, having employees act without some kind of checks and balances is a recipe for disaster. So how do fast growth companies compensate for this?

Answer: they anticipate the potential pitfalls and create systems that guide individuals to make right choices (and avoid making the wrong ones). For example, a common problem in a lot of small businesses is that staff members will often make expense decisions without ever checking cash flow. To avoid this, most small business leaders have very low dollar amounts that their staff members can expense without approval. Yet, interestingly, the Ritz Carlton empowers their cleaning staff with the power to fix any problem up to $500 without approval. Isn't that amazing? I know a number of leaders who won't let their college-educated top team members make a $500 decision without their approval.

But more importantly, what does the typical small business CEO do when they see a large expense item? Exactly! One of the first things they do is check cash flow. And the second is they check the YTD budget figures for that staff member's area. So let me ask you, "Why can't a staff member do those same two checks themselves?" If they did, they would save you both the time and effort from doing so and enable you to stay focused on the projects you need to be focused on.

In other words, what fast growth companies do to ensure fast execution is make sure they've set up all the systems and guidelines necessary to guide their individual staff members to make the right decisions — without having to continually check with other people. By removing all of the hindrances to action, they've, by definition, sped up the process of taking action.

2. **Empowerment**

Following on the heels of number one, fast growth companies are very proactive about empowerment. They're driven, not by the need to control, but by the desire to leverage their people for the greatest impact possible. This is why they always delegate both authority and responsibility to their people. One without the other makes no sense.

However, in slow growth and plateaued companies, we see exactly the opposite. Slow growth leaders tend to delegate only the responsibility, not the authority, which is why their people have to continually get approval from those above them to take new action or to make big decisions. Why? Because, if they're honest, slow growth leaders don't really trust their people. If they did, they'd transfer both the authority and the responsibility hand-in-hand.

Fast growth leaders, on the other hand, trust their people and believe that they'll do the right thing — which is why they have no problem at all with delegating both authority and responsibility. It's all about trust!

3. **Modeling fast action**

Leaders of fast growth businesses know that the phrase, "People do what people see," is just as valid today as it has been throughout history. That's why they make sure they're continually modeling fast execution in their own lives.

Nido Qubein, the President of High Point University, who has built and sold several businesses, is also the chairman of Great Harvest Bread Company, sits on the board of BB&T, consults several companies, does 40 outside speaking engagements per year, teaches a class on campus each semester, and coaches speakers. How? By taking fast action.

Nido breaks his days down into five minute "units." If you ask him, "Can we get together for an hour?" he'll say, "That's twelve units!" Nido gets things done. And that modeling has caught on. In his first six years at High Point, Nido has lead a $550M renovation and expansion of the campus that is truly remarkable (on the way to a $2.1B renovation). It's a transformation that has turned a small Methodist college into US News & World Report's number one up and coming college in the South. Things happen fast at HPU. Why? Because they have a leader who models fast action every single day.

4. **A culture of action**

In fast growth companies, it's not just the leader who

models fast execution, it's the entire organization. It's almost visceral. The entire culture of the business is organized, not around debate and delay or CYA, but around empowerment and fast execution. Fast growth companies are always seeking to narrow the gap between the inception of an idea and its execution.

John Masters, a Canadian Hunter, puts it this way.

> *"This is so simple it sounds stupid, but it is amazing how few oil people really understand that you only find oil if you drill wells. You may think you're finding it when you're drawing maps and studying log books, but you actually have to drill."*

John is right. Though his advice sounds so obvious, it's amazing how few businesses or organizations actually practice it. In fact, I've found very few organizations that have a culture with a bias towards fast execution. Yet, if you want to break through your plateau and get back on a growth curve, you've got to create a culture of execution where everyone knows, "We get things done fast around here."

So, how can you go about creating that kind of culture? Well, here are a few ideas to help you increase the speed of implementation in your business (or organization).

1. **Reward quick action.**

   As the old saying goes, "What gets rewarded gets done." So create a series of awards for people who act fast. You could give awards on the spot for fast execution (maybe a gift card to John because he left the meeting on Tuesday and acted on his assignment immediately). Or you could create a monthly award for the person who generated the most activity. Or you could ... Be creative. Have fun. But make sure your people know that speed matters!

   Note: You don't have to do this forever. You might choose to create a six or twelve-month campaign to increase the speed of implementation in your business and then move on to another issue.

2. **Reward risk-taking and fast prototyping**

If you want to create a fast executing organization, then you've got to eliminate or minimize the fear of failure your employees possess.

One of my favorite quotes of all-time comes from an Australian businessman, Phil Daniels, who reduced his philosophy of management down to six simple words,

"Reward excellent failures. Punish mediocre successes."

I love that! In fact, in my previous career, I used to say to my staff and lay leaders frequently, "Listen, if you're willing to go out and try something bold and risky — and it fails miserably. Don't worry. I'll be the first in line to congratulate you for taking a risk. However, if you're not willing to do that and instead choose to play it safe and nothing goes wrong, don't expect me to come running up and say, "Great job!" Because I won't. In fact, I may get on your case because you chose to play it safe."

Another great line on this subject comes from David Kelly, the creative CEO of IDEO, who once said,

"Fail faster. Succeed sooner."

3. **Simplify and eliminate any policies, procedures or processes that hinder speed.**

Every organization has them. They may be old systems. They may be checks and balances systems. They may be industry standards. But you do have them. Inefficiency is present in every organization.

The problem with this, as you learned in science class years ago, is that whenever you have drag/friction/inefficiency, the speed of an object in motion always slows down-which means that as soon as you remove whatever's causing the drag, you'll immediately increase the speed of that object (through your system).

4. **Keep pushing authority and responsibility down the chain.**

One of the primary responsibilities of leadership, which we'll come back to in the next chapter is leverage. But you can't leverage your people well if your people don't have both the responsibility and authority to act—especially apart from your approval. So if you want to create a fast growth culture, then you've got to keep pushing authority and responsibility as far down the chain as you can.

In addition, when someone with whom you've delegated authority and responsibility to comes to you and asks for your opinion—you've got to resist the temptation to weigh in—or you'll keep reinforcing a slow growth culture. Whenever anyone to whom you've delegated authority and responsibility comes and asks for your approval, make sure you say, "Hey, I gave you the authority and responsibility to make the call, you make it!"

Note: this doesn't mean you can't ever voice your opinion or mentor your people. What it means is that you don't want your people to remain dependent upon you. You don't want them to slow down the process of implementation until they can check with you. Nor do you want to create a leader who's afraid to make tough calls on their own.

So use your best judgment. And stay aware. Most of us like to voice our opinions (after all, we are the senior leader), but we rarely think about the consequences of doing so. If you want your people to execute fast, then make sure you keep empowering them to make the tough calls by refusing to weigh in yourself.

5. **Set time limits on discussion**

In order to create more ownership and buy in (or because of fear or lack of confidence), a lot of leaders will allow a lot of executive discussions to go on for way too long (weeks, months, and sometimes even years) rather than force them to decide and execute.

A simple, quick, easy-to-use practice that can help you avoid that problem is to set time limits on discussions at the beginning. For example, let's say you're discussing a new marketing strategy, "Should we add an offline direct mail campaign to supplement our online Google Adwords campaign?" While some companies would discuss this for weeks/months, you might start out your meeting by saying, "Okay, we've got 30 minutes to discuss this today after which we're going to make a decision." Simply by making that one change you'll immediately increase the speed of implementation in your business.

6. **Review how you personally contribute to slowing down implementation.**

    Remember, "People do what people see." If you don't like what you see out there (meaning in your people or in your organization), then you always want to start by taking a look at the part you play.

    If you don't get your assignments done between staff meetings, how can you get frustrated with your staff members who don't get theirs done? Or if you don't return your phone calls or respond to emails quickly, how can you be frustrated when your people don't either? Or if you don't hit your deadlines (or better, beat them), how can you be upset with your people when they don't hit theirs?

    In other words, if you want to create a fast executing organization, then you need to model fast execution in your own life. The sooner you do that, the sooner your people will change and, in fact, the entire culture of your organization will change.

So, if you'd like to break through your plateau and build a bigger, better, faster and more profitable business, then I'd encourage you to start right here with Driver #1: Speed of Implementation. Of all the drivers, this one truly is number one for a reason. If you want to grow faster, you've got to implement faster. Period. There are no ifs, ands, or buts available. It just is.

Applying Driver #1: Speed of Implementation

1. On a scale of 1-10 (high), how would you rate your business (or organization) on its speed of implementation?

   _____

2. On a scale of 1-10 (high), how would you rate yourself on your speed of implementation? _____

3. Which of the four causes of analysis paralysis are you and your business most affected by? And what have been the impacts those causes have had on your company?

4. What is one thing you can do to decrease analysis paralysis?

5. Which of the four contributors to fast execution do you need to focus more attention on?

6. What can you do to ensure that that contributor increases your speed?

7. What do you need to do to better model fast execution?

8. Were there any other ideas that came to mind as you read this chapter that could help you create a better culture of fast execution?

9. What would you say is your major takeaway from this chapter?

10. What is one thing you can do within the next 48-72 hours to increase the speed of implementation in your business?

"The most important word in the world of money is cash flow. The second most important word is leverage."

Robert Kiyosaki, author *Rich Dad, Poor Dad*

Chapter 2
"Do Less, Accomplish More"

Driver #2: Leverage

My guess is that you're pretty familiar with Archimedes' famous statement about leverage.

> *"Give me a lever long enough and a fulcrum on which to place it, and I shall move the world."* Archimedes

The problem, of course, is that while most entrepreneurial leaders like the idea or concept of leverage generically, very few like the actual practice of executing the concept specifically. If you don't believe me, let me prove it to you.

Read through the following series of statements. After each statement, either mentally or physically, check off whether or not you've thought or made the following statement recently. For example,

- ❑ *"No one can do it as well as I can"*
- ❑ *"They never get it done right."*
- ❑ *"I can get it done faster if I just do it myself."*
- ❑ *"This is my business. I'm the one who's supposed to make the decisions."*
- ❑ *" I don't want anyone screwing up my business."*

❑　*"I don't want anyone taking my business away from me (or taking it in another direction)."*
❑　*"The only person I can really trust is me."*

So, how many of those statements did you check off? If you're like most of the entrepreneurial leaders I know, you probably checked off at least five (or more) — and that's a problem. Why? Because beliefs influence behavior. If you're thinking, "I can get it done faster if I just do it myself," what do you think the probability is that you're going to delegate that task and leverage someone else's time and effort? And that's a bigger problem than most leaders want to admit — especially those who need to break through a plateau and get back on a growth curve.

Why? Because leadership is all about leverage — and leverage is what creates the potential for growth. The only reason any leader should ever hire an additional person is to create leverage — to create a greater result than could have been achieved by that individual alone.

In fact, the whole notion of leadership is based upon the presupposition that a leader can generate a synergy with a team of people that will produce a better outcome than the sum of those individual team members' efforts. Or to put it another way, if a "leader" isn't creating leverage, they're not leading.

On the other hand, what leaders of fast growth companies know is that if they want to achieve growth at an accelerated pace, they've got to create leverage. And specifically, they're looking to create leverage through four primary means.

1.　**Other people's time and effort (OPT)**

While this is the most obvious and common form of leverage, it also means that the higher the quality of talent you have on your team, the better the leverage you can create. So if Frank is an average manager and Angelo is a great manager, the more "Angelo's" you hire, the more leverage you create. However, the opposite is also true. The more "Frank's" you hire (or currently have on your team), the lower the amount of leverage you can create — which is what tends to be true for plateaued businesses and organization.

But this problem goes even deeper. In fact, one of the primary reasons why so many small business leaders struggle with leveraging other people's time and effort is because they tend to think that if they can do something — they should. You may have fallen prey to this same kind of thinking yourself. "Why pay someone else to do what I can do?"

The problem with that kind of thinking is that if you value your time at, let's say, $100/hour, any task that you spend time on that delivers less than that amount of value is an underleveraged moment. Moreover, if you were to hire someone at $20 an hour to take care of the vast majority of your administrivia (which is definitely not a $100 hour task), you would not have only made a good business decision — you would have also created leverage.

In addition, by hiring someone to focus on your administrivia, you will have created the space you need to focus on those activities that can generate real revenue for your business. Or to put it another way, by leveraging someone else's time (at a lower price point), you can create leverage for yourself and your business to grow faster.

2. **Other people's intellectual property/expertise/talent (OPIP)**

Another one of the major hindrances to accelerated growth is the rugged individualism of our American past. The desire for owners and entrepreneurs to want to say, "I did it myself," or, "I made it happen," is disruptive to the very essence of leverage and leadership.

If you struggle with this whole concept, one of the most important questions you need to ask yourself is, "Why?" For example, "Why do I feel the need to be in control of everything?" Or, "Why do I feel the need to be able to say, 'I did it myself!'" Or, "Why do I need to know this?" Or, "Why do I struggle with letting someone else run this?" Or, "Why am I afraid to admit I don't know how to do something?"

These are the kinds of questions — and their subsequent answers — that can unlock a whole new growth pattern for you and your company. Why? Because leaders of fast growth companies don't need to control everything (or know everything). They have no problem with finding good people who know things they don't know or who are better than them at something. In fact, they hire those people — as employees, consultants, outsourcers, and even as board members — so they can create real leverage — which is essential to growth (especially double-digit growth).

Leaders who always have to be right or who always need to be, "the smartest person in the room," will continually struggle with leverage. In light of that, may I encourage you … don't be that person!

You want to be the leader who surrounds himself or herself with highly talented individuals who are better than you are at whatever they're great at. If you're not a great money manager, get a great CFO or accountant who possess intellectual property that you don't. Or if you want to go national, but don't know the ins and outs of creating and launching a retail franchise, bring someone on your team (or board) who brings that kind of expertise and leverage their intellectual property.

As a leader who wants to create leverage, why should you ever be afraid of genius? You want to be surrounded by a whole team of incredibly talented individuals! The better they are, the better you are. Furthermore, being the smartest person in the room is a terrible objective for a leader. Why? Because it's entirely self-focused — which is something that should never be your focus as a leader. Great leaders are always on a talent hunt, looking for great people (with unique intellectual property) that they can leverage in order to create a greater result.

3. **Other people's money (OPM)**

    If you want to grow a fast growth business or organization, there will be a number of times when you're going to need to access more cash than either you have on hand or that you can generate internally. While internally generated cash is preferable to borrowed capital for the normal running of a business, if you want to grow faster, chances are you'll need to leverage the capital of others.

    For example, let's go back to the example in chapter one of hiring an additional sales person. Few sales people pay for themselves right off the bat. Usually, there's a training period, followed by a developmental period. However, at some point in the future, dependent upon your sales cycle, the revenue that

that new sales person generates should surpass the expense they create — and do so for years. However, to get to that point, most companies usually need to leverage the money of others to create the cash flow they need in the short-term until their new investment pays off.

That said, there's nothing wrong with trying to grow through internally generated cash. However, when it comes to accelerated growth, internally generated cash is usually a growth limiter. In fact, if you want to read an excellent article about this subject, check out Neil Churchill's excellent article on, *"How Fast Can Your Company Afford to Grow?"* (Harvard Business Review, May 2001, pp. 135-142). The formula he lays out is easy to follow. But it'll also tell you at what rate your internally generated cash will max out at. If you want to grow faster than that, you'll definitely need to leverage other people's money (OPM)

4. **Other people's networks (OPN)**

Why would you ever want to limit your reach to only the people who you know or the people in your network know? One of the great observations that Linkedin affords (to anyone who has a Linkedin account) is the ability to see that our reach is much greater than we believe it is.

For example, you may think, "I only know a few people" (let's say 75). However, each of those people knows a number of people whom you don't know (for simplicities sake, let's say 75 people x your original 75, which equals 5,625). And each of those people knows people you don't know either (again, let's say 75 people x 5,625 people, which equals 421,875 people in your network — just two levels away from you). Of course, the cool part about Linkedin is that you don't have to do the math — the software does it for you!

Having said that, you and I both know that knowing something and doing it are two completely different things. While most leaders "know" this concept, few exploit it. What differentiates fast growth leaders from others is that they act on this principle immediately. They actually leverage their relationships. They use them to get contacts and referrals. They use their network to get projects done. And they use their network to eliminate obstacles and cut through red tape.

In other words, fast growth leaders not only "get it" that leveraging other people's networks is essential to growing their business faster, they do it.

So, if you'd like to do a better job at creating more leverage for yourself and your business so that you can break through your plateau and build a bigger, better, faster and more profitable business (or organization), here are a few thoughts on how you can do that.

1. **Change your belief system**.

    One of the most difficult transitions any leader has to make when they become a leader is realizing that their own success is no longer dependent upon their performance, but upon the performance of the people they're leading.

    At first this seems like a cruel hoax. The reason most leaders become leaders is because they're good at getting something done. Then, the moment they become a leader it's like someone pulls the carpet out from underneath them and says, "Ha! Ha! It's no longer about you and what you can do!"

    From that moment on, your "job performance" should no longer be judged based on what you do, but based on what your people do. This is a radically different way of thinking than most leaders think. If you don't believe me, let me prove it to you.

    Take a look at your calendar for the past week or two. How much of your time did you spend coaching or helping your direct reports? Then, how much time did you spend focused on what you needed to do?

    Or when you get to the end of the year and you evaluate your own performance — do you start by looking at what you accomplished ... or what your direct reports accomplished? If you're like most owners, entrepreneurs and service providers I know, your answer is the former. Why? Because of your belief system (i.e. what you believe to be true about leadership and what leaders do).

    In other words, what I'm suggesting is that if you want to create better leverage, you have to make sure your belief system about leadership is in line with what true leadership is all about. True leadership is all about producing results through other people. It's not about what the leader does. It's about what the people they're leading accomplish. Once you own that belief, it'll literally change everything for you and your business.

2. **Design your business so that everyone wins**

Most owners like to lead companies that generate the greatest amount of cash possible for their own pockets. Now, there's nothing wrong with wanting to make a lot of money.

But, if you want to lead and leverage a team of talented individuals, you need to create a business where they win as well. Why? Because when everyone has some skin in the game, it's amazing how much harder they'll work. In fact, a great book on this subject is, "The Great Game of Business," by Jack Stack.

I love this book for a number of reasons, but one of them is that it's a mind-expanding book. Listen, if a remanufacturing company on the fast track to closing down can redesign how they reward employees so much so that the guy on an assembly line is making a decision, "Should I take the time to remake this part or put in a new part?" based on the financial implications of his hourly rate vs. the cost of a new part because he wants to share in the biggest bonus pool possible, then don't you think you can do the same in your business?

One of the most freeing and leverage producing questions you can ever ask yourself is, "How can I design this business in such a way that everyone wins?"

A fellow speaker, Stephen Shapiro made a comment one time that fits perfectly here. He said, "While in Asia, I heard a great expression, "Before You Can Multiply, You Must First Learn to Divide." I now find myself using this saying nearly every day. The idea is that if you want to grow your business, you must learn to partner with others – and give them a slice. This means you take a smaller slice of a bigger pie."

3. **Recruit only A players**.

When it comes to leverage, the team with the best talent wins! Unfortunately, most small businesses and organizations have more than a few B, C and D players on their team. And the reality is, you can't create an A team, with B, C, and D players.

In other words, one of the fastest ways you can create more leverage — and speed up the growth of your business — is to transition out some of your C and D players. Once you've done that, you'll have the space and capital to recruit and replace them with A players.

The bottom line is that if you want to break through your plateau and build a bigger, better, faster and more profitable business, then you've got to make a commitment to only recruiting A players — and to not letting pressure or workload get in the way so that you'll cave in and hire another C or D player. You have to believe at the very core of your being that you can only create an A team with A players. So, do you?

4. **Make sure everyone is working in their sweet spot**

    Whenever you or I hire someone, there's usually an implicit assumption that the position we're hiring them for is the best position for them.

    However, it's not until they're actually in the job, doing the work, that we actually know whether or not that position is the best fit for them. Unfortunately, what tends to happen in most small businesses is that they tend to keep the people they hire in the same positions that they originally hired them for — regardless of whether or not that position is the best fit for the person they hired.

    Note: This is true of both good performers as well as well as poor performers, but let's focus on the poor performers first since they're the more common of the two. It's not unusual to find that someone you've hired — who's underperforming, let's say at inside sales — may, in fact, be a great at something else, let's say, online marketing or SEO. In other words, just because someone isn't perfect for a certain position doesn't automatically mean you should let them go.

    On the other hand, with good performers, you should never assume that just because someone is good at something that they're in their sweet spot — because they may not be. This is an optimization question, which we'll come to in chapter three, but for now, I'm confident you grasp the idea that good performance may be the enemy of great performance. Just because you hired Anik as your CFO (which he's good at), doesn't mean you're getting the best leverage out of him. He may in fact be a great marketer who could take your company to a whole new level.

Or to put it another way, if you want to better leverage the time, talents and intellectual property of your people, you have to diligently know them inside out so that you can ensure that they're all in their sweet spots.

5. **Invest significantly in staff training**.

This principle flows directly off the A player principle. If it's true (and it is) that the better your people are, the more leverage they create, then it stands to reason that investing significantly in training and development is one of the best uses of your time, effort and money.

One of the major mistakes a lot of small business leaders make is that they tend to minimize the amount of time they personally invest in developing their people. Secondly, they don't invest enough time and money in staff development, as a whole. And thirdly, when economic times get tough they almost always cut the training and development budget first— which is exactly the opposite of what they should do.

When times are tough, you need your people performing at a higher level. But how are they going to get there without help? Apart from continually investing in training and development, you can only expect that they'll simply continue to deliver the same kinds of results that they have in the past (at best). To expect anything different is pure foolishness.

If you want your people to perform at a higher level (and as the leader of a plateaued business, you need them to perform at a higher level), then you need to personally help them get there. Back when Jack Welch was at GE, even though he was the CEO of a global Fortune 500 company, he used to devote one day a week, every other week, to developing leaders. Is there any wonder why GE, under Welch, was such a fast growth company during his tenure? Or why when so many of his protégés were picked by other companies to be CEOs at theirs.

Noel Tichy, who worked with Jack during those years, put it this way.

"Winning companies win because they have good leaders who nurture the development of other leaders at all levels of the organization."

So if you really want to break through your current plateau and get back on a double-digit growth curve, you'll want to make sure that you're creating leverage at every level and at every position in your organization or business. Why? Because the more leverage you create, the faster your business (or organization) will grow.

Applying Driver #2: Leverage

1. On a scale of 1-10 (high), how would you rate yourself on leveraging each of the four points of leveraging other people

    a. Leveraging other people's time and effort?

        _____

    b. Leveraging other people's intellectual property?

        _____

    c. Leveraging other people's money?

        _____

    d. Leveraging other people's networks?

        _____

2. What do you think hinders you from better leveraging your people?

3. Who are the underperformers (your C and D players) in your business (or organization)?

4. What are you going to do with each of them (Develop, Move, or Remove)?

5. Who do you need to add to your team? Or, what positions do you need to add to your team to accelerate your business' growth?

6. Read Neil Churchill's article on "How Fast Can Your Company Grow?" Then do the calculations for your own business.

7. Whose network do you need to leverage (or better leverage)? How?

8. Which of the leverage application ideas do you need to apply? How?

9. What is your major takeaway from this chapter?

10. What is one thing you can do within the next week to better leverage some of the people on your team?

Chapter 3
"Tweak, Test, and Repeat"

Driver #3: Optimization

Before you gag and skip this chapter (I know, the idea of optimization usually causes a gag reflux in the lives of most entrepreneurs), hang with me for just a moment. The reason you probably picked up this book is because A. you want to grow your business or organization faster and B. that's currently not happening (or, at least, not happening as fast as you'd like).

Now, while there are a number of reasons why that may be true, one of the possible reasons why is because whenever a business owner or entrepreneur is confronted with a plateau or a lack of growth, their first solution to the problem is to go out and acquire more customers or clients.

While there's nothing inherently wrong with going out and acquiring more customers or clients, the fundamental problem with that strategy is that the fastest and easiest way to increase your revenues and profits isn't by throwing more money at client acquisition — but rather in obtaining more from your current customers. Once you achieve that, you can then take the same amount of money that you were investing in your marketing efforts and, by using a process to optimize your results, you can increase your results (i.e. make more money) without increasing your investment dollars.

In other words, growing your business faster, doesn't always mean, "Invest a lot more money." In fact, I would argue that it's far better to optimize your efforts with your current clients first and then to optimize your client attraction strategies, than it is to just throw more money at client acquisition.

You see, the good news about optimization (even if you're not a fan of the word) is that it simply means, "To get a better result from your efforts without incurring any additional cost, time or resources." How can you not like that?

For example, if your current clients spend $5,000 a year with you, why be content with that? What if you could increase their average transactional size? Or their frequency of purchase? What if you could optimize your current customers so they bought six times a year instead of five? Or what if they bought $1,100 per purchase instead of $1,000? Or what if they did both? What would those changes mean to your bottom line? My guess is that they'd be huge. Now, do I have your attention?

Or let's take a look at your marketing efforts. Let's say you're currently sending out a direct mail piece to 10,000 people once a quarter. Since you're already sending out 10,000 pieces once per quarter, how much more does it cost you to optimize your results by testing out a different headline to half of the people you're already sending a direct mail piece to? Nothing.

Once you grasp that, here's how optimization can help you get your business off your current plateau. Instead of mailing 10,000 of the same direct mail pieces with the same headline to the same 10,000 people, what if you sent 5,000 pieces out with headline A (the one you've been using) to 5,000 people and 5,000 pieces out with headline B (the headline you want to test) to the remaining 5,000 people on your list?

Assuming that you're measuring the results of your marketing efforts, lets' say that headline A (the one you've been using) gets a response rate of 1% (not bad, but not earthshattering either) and headline B (your test headline) gets a response rate of 3% (pretty significant). How much more did it cost you to get that 3X response rate? Nothing. In other words, for no additional cost, you now know how to triple your response rate.

This is what makes optimization so incredibly amazing. You're already spending the money to send out 10,000 direct mail pieces once a quarter (and, if you're like most owners and entrepreneurs, you're basically sending out the same piece to the same people, year after year). But by taking the time to simply test a headline (i.e. to optimize it) your response rate has now shot up by 300%! What that means is that if you had sent out all 10,000 pieces with Headline B, you would have received 200 more leads than you normally do — for no additional cost! Hooked yet?

But, it gets even better. Headline B is now your new control (the New Headline A) and if you keep testing that headline against new Headline Bs you might be able to optimize your 3% response rate to a 4% or 5% (or higher). And how much more does this cost you? Absolutely nothing. You were already spending the money to send out 10,000 direct mail pieces every quarter anyways.

Now, while the basic idea of optimization is pretty easy to grasp and while the implementation of it is pretty simple, most entrepreneurs stink at it. Why? For two primary reasons.

1. As I mentioned before, the natural temptation for most entrepreneurs is to continually focus their attention on attracting more new customers (even though the quickest and least expensive way to grow is by optimizing revenue from current customers). It's almost hypnotic. The siren song of, "Attract more customers," often overrides the more mundane but profitable call to generate more revenue from current customers — which is unfortunate. As to why this is so common, my guess is that it's probably driven by the entrepreneurial desire to do or create something new.

2. Most entrepreneurs dislike the whole managerial, creating systems, data collection processes that are required in order to obtain an optimized result. It's anathema to them! So they tend to avoid it.

However, if you want to improve your effort at anything, by definition, you can't know if you've improved that effort unless you have a quantifiable result against which you can measure your new result. Or to put it another way, how can you know if the result you're now obtaining is better than a previous result — unless you have some quantifiable way to justify that conclusion.

In general, most entrepreneurs don't want to do this. Why? Because, most entrepreneurs prefer to go by their gut. You can hear it all the time when they say something like, "I think we should do [blank]" When you ask them, "Why?" How do they typically respond, "Because." Or, "I just know." If you ask them for some data or proof, they'll usually scoff at you and say something like, "I don't have time to gather all that data crap!"

But, as we've just seen, by NOT taking the time to gather data and optimize results, most business leaders are leaving massive amounts of money on the table. I'm all for leading by the gut. In fact, on my last personality type inventory I scored a perfect 30/30 on intuition. However, I also know that data is essential to making wise decisions — especially when it comes to increasing productivity and results.

In fact, this is one of the primary ways that management adds real value to any organization — especially an accelerated growth business. By designing, testing and evaluating the resulting data, management allows any business to deliver better results with the same (or fewer) resources.

This is especially true when it comes to your marketing and sales functions — which are essential if you want to get up off your current plateau and back on a double-digit growth curve. Going back to our earlier example in this chapter, if you were to simply spend the same amount of money that you're currently spending on your marketing and sales — but you were to use an optimized tactic (that brings about a tripling of your response rate), wouldn't it make sense that optimization alone could accelerate the growth of your business? Absolutely!

Or let's take your current sales script. Let's say your current sales script is converting at a 20% rate (i.e. 20% of your leads convert to sales), what would it be worth to you if you could test a few changes in your script and start converting at a 40% or 60% rate? If you do the math, you could possibly double or triple your annual revenues just by optimizing your sales script. And how much does that cost you? Absolutely nothing!

Now, my experience with owners and entrepreneurs may be skewed (i.e. a referent group of one (me) is not statistically significant), but I've found virtually no owners or entrepreneurs who regularly engage in testing (that is, apart from online marketers). So, to make this chapter as valuable and as practical as possible, rather than discuss more sophisticated multi-variant testing, let's talk about what's known as A/B Testing.

An A/B test is the kind of test I shared with you earlier in this chapter. You take a new thing (the B) and you test it against an old thing (the A—also known as the "control"). In the example above I tested the headline of our direct mail piece, but we just as easily could have tested any part of our offer. For example, we could have tested the price, the times, the bonuses, the benefits, the testimonials, the endorsements, the text copy, the guarantee, the urgency tactic, etc.

Continuing in this vein, let's test price this time. Let's say you just created a product that you think has a value of at least $197. You could send an offer to one half of your list with a price of, let's say, $197 (that would be Price A). Then you could send an offer to the other half of your list with a price of $297 (Price B). What might surprise you is that the $297 price just might outsell the $197—even though it's the exact same product.

In other words, if you're not constantly testing and optimizing your marketing and sales activities, including things like price, you're leaving money on the table. To see how quickly this can add up, you'll want to check out the table you're about to encounter—but first, there are a few things you need to know in order to appreciate the table.

When it comes to generating more revenue, there are three primary levers you can pull. You can increase the number of clients or customers who buy from you; you can increase the average amount of each transaction; and/or you can increase the frequency of purchase.

In the following table, you'll notice that by simply keeping the same number of customers (in the first two examples), but increasing the average transaction size and frequency of purchase (two optimizing functions) by just 10%, you could generate an additional $210,000 (all from your current customers—i.e. you really are leaving money on the table). If you then extend that 10% increase to optimizing your marketing efforts to new customers as well, you could easily generate an additional $121,000 (for a total increase of $331,000).

# of clients	x	Avg. trans. size	x	Freq. of purchase	=	Revenue
100	x	$5000	x	2	=	$1,000,000
100	x	$5500	x	2.2	=	$1,210,000
110	x	$5500	x	2.2	=	$1,331,000

In other words, you can't afford to not add more optimization to your business or organization. So, how do you make this happen? Well, here are a few more thoughts.

1. **Start by collecting data on whatever you want to optimize**

    As you read above, you can't optimize anything unless you have a result against which you can compare the new result — which means that the first step to optimizing anything is to create a benchmark. It doesn't matter what the thing is that you want to optimize, you just have to have a result to compare your new result against.

    For example, if you want to optimize the number of opt ins on your website, then you need to know how many people are currently visiting your site each month and then what percentage of them are giving you their email address or calling you. Likewise, if you want to increase the number of referrals from your staff, you need to get a benchmark for how frequently they're asking and how many referrals they're generating.

2. **Decide what part you want to test**

    If it's a marketing piece, do you want to test the headline? Or the price? Or the bonuses? Or the payment options? Or the upsell? Or the guarantee? Or the testimonials? What do you want to test?

    Whatever you decide to test — and this is important — you should only test one thing at a time. Why? Because if you make multiple changes (let's say you change the headline, the price, the benefits, two pictures, the guarantee, and two testimonials), you won't know which one made the difference (was it the headline? Or the guarantee? Or the testimonials? Or the price?). Apart from testing only one variable at a time, you and I just can't know for sure. So only test one part of your offer at a time (or one piece of whatever you're testing — like one piece of a performance review system).

    Remember: You can optimize just about anything in your business. Even though we're focused on customer acquisition and maximizing customer value in these examples, you can still use this same basic process for anything (i.e. you could test the speed of customer fulfillment).

3. **Run the test**

    Whatever it is you want to test, test it. And then make sure you collect the data. How many people called from your ad A vs. ad B in the paper? How many new leads went to the website and filled in the form from Google ad A vs. Google ad B? How many referrals came from your front desk staff when they used script A vs. script B?

4. **Compare the data**

    Once you've completed your A/B test, you need to compare your new data against your old data to see which one returned the better result. If B out performs A, then B becomes your new control (the New A).

5. **Keep testing other variables**

    For example, let's go back to our price test — and let's use the price of $297 as our new control (since, in our imaginary test, it beat out $197). You can now test other prices to see if they get better results, but you can also test other pricing issues like a payment plan over a one-time payment to see which gets a better result. In this case, your original B is now your A ($297), and your B is now a payment plan (three payments of $99). If A wins, it remains the control. But if the payment plan wins, then B becomes the new A (the control). The next thing you may want to test is something else in the offer — like maybe a 30-day trial for $2.95 (versus the three pay plan).

The possibilities are endless, but the key to being great at optimizing is realizing that there is no finish line in testing. There's always something you can or should be testing that could increase your response rate.

Which means that, if your business or organization is plateaued and you want to get back on a double-digit growth curve, you'll definitely want to unleash growth driver #3 (optimization) to help you build that bigger, better, faster and more profitable business or organization you long for.

Applying Driver #3: Optimization

1. On a scale of 1-10 (high), how would you rate yourself on optimizing your business and its offers? Why?

   7-8

2. What do you think hinders you from investing more time and energy on optimizing what you're currently doing?

   ideas

   already made changes

   not a risk taker

3. How do you think your personal feelings about optimization have affected your business (or organization)? Be specific.

   doer not thinker!

4. What was the last thing you tested? What were the results?

   telephone system

5. If you were to focus more time and energy on optimizing your marketing and sales efforts, what do you think that would be worth to you?

6. What do you think is the first thing you should test in order to optimize a result?

7. How will you conduct the test? When?

8. What is your major takeaway from this chapter?

   Measure - Measure

9. What is one thing you can do within the next week to better optimize your efforts to either increase the current value of your current customers or attract more new customers to your business (or organization)?

   I'm good at asking questions.
   I don't stick with — because we
   always did it that way.
   I'm always looking for ways
   to improve.

"Nothing can add more power to your life than concentrating all your energies on a limited set of targets."

Nido Qubein, President of High Point University, Philanthropist, and Horatio Alger's Award Winner

Chapter 4
"Stop Trying to Move 50 Things Down the Field at Once"

Driver # 4: Focus

As you look back on your life, when have you been the most productive?

- When you've had a massive list of "to do" items? Or a short list of "to do" items?
- When you've tried to accomplish ten or more strategic initiatives in a year? Or when you've tried to accomplish one to three strategic initiatives within a year?
- When you've attempted to generate leads through ten different channels? Or when you've attempted to generate leads through three proven channels?

In one sense, the answers to those question seem so blatantly obvious that they shouldn't even need to be asked. However, the reality is that the vast majority of business leaders are far better at spraying than they are at focusing — at trying to do too many things in too many directions, rather than focusing on a few things in a few directions. And this is true at every level of business size — from Fortune 500 companies to Inc. 500 companies, even down to solo-practitioners.

For example, a friend of mine and I used to meet about once a month for several years at Panera Bread (we now meet online) and we frequently ended up revisiting this driver. Why? Because often when we get together he'd hand me a new business card with a new name for his existing business, or a new name for a new business, or a new idea for a new product that he was working on that was unrelated to any of his other core businesses.

Even though he intellectually knew that what he was doing was wrong, he couldn't help himself—which is why, whenever we were together, I often found myself taking my two hands, extending them out wide, and then bringing them to the center at the same time I kept repeating, "Focus. Focus. Focus."

And he's not alone. Most of us, as entrepreneurial leaders, struggle with this issue—and for a number of reasons.

1. **We live in a world that values options**.

    As such, it just makes sense to us that if we come up with lots of ideas for what we can do or if we can offer our customers and prospects lots of options, that's clearly better than having/offering fewer options—since more is clearly better than less (or so we think). In other words, the whole idea of focusing on a few options seems almost antithetical to our worldview that "More is better than less."

2. **We think we can do more than we can**

    As highly driven entrepreneurial leaders, we almost always think we can do more than is humanly possible. We fill up our "to do" lists with too many items because, "Well, we can get more done than the average Joe (or Jane)." Or we say, "Yes!" to too many requests because we actually believe, "We can always add one more thing to our plate and still get done what we need to get done on time." Even worse, for many of us, the whole idea of "focusing," seems like a rather weak practice and a cop out for not being able to execute quickly.

3. **We think that if someone wants to give us money, we should take it.**

Now, there's nothing wrong with wanting to make more money. But what tends to happen with most owners and entrepreneurs of small and medium-sized businesses is that they easily veer from their focused markets or products or core competencies simply because someone comes along and says, "Hey, I'll pay you 'x' if you'll do 'y' for me. "

In one sense, this seems like a harmless thing to do. Just say, "Yes!" to cash. But it is harmful for a number of reasons. For example, whenever a decision takes a business or organization away from its core focused strategy, that's usually a bad thing.

Or whenever a business tries to do too many things, it usually ends up creating a branding and marketing problem (i.e. what exactly is the brand of a company that does everything?).

However, to me, the greatest danger of this "too many options" approach is that it hinders customer buying behavior. For example, there's a restaurant near where I live called Roy's Place. Roy's offers 228 different sandwiches, plus dinners, plus salads. My wife ate there exactly ONCE. It took her FOREVER to make a decision. Why? Because too many options made it difficult to decide.

Which means that, from an owner's perspective, you should never want to offer too many options because offering too many options creates confusion — and as all good sales people know — a confused mind is a non-buying mind.

I experienced this not too long ago myself. I needed to buy a new sliding glass door for the doorway leading out to our patio. After visiting the two big box home stores (Lowes and Home Depot) I decided to give a local supplier an option at getting my business (I'm pro local businesses). So I walked in, explained what I was looking for and was handed a nice 11" x 17" four panel full color brochure for a door that would run about $1500. I then asked if there was a less expensive option and he handed me a brochure for a door that would run around $750.

When I got home I opened up the two brochures. The one showing the $1500 door was clearly a better door with lots of great options — ten colors of this, five options for that, seven options for handles, eight options for this, etc. Then I opened up the brochure for the $750 door. There were just three options of color and three options of handles. And guess what? Even though I knew the $1500 door would be better, the number of options they presented me with required more from me than I was willing to invest. I simply wanted a new sliding glass door—and the simplicity of the choices that the cheaper door offered won my heart over. Remember, more is not always better.

Likewise, when it comes to offering more products or services, every owner and/or entrepreneur needs to constantly be aware that the more products and/or services their business offers, the more their brand is diluted.

4. We get bored

Let's be honest, as entrepreneurial leaders, most of us have a preferential bent toward starting things, rather than finishing them. We like the thrill of chasing an idea or coming up with the next new thing as opposed to the routine-ness of staying focused and on task with something that's already been decided--over an extended period of time.

But regardless of why you struggle with focus, if you want to break through your plateau and get back on a double-digit growth curve, you've got to make focus one of the core drivers of you business. Why? Because focus matters

You can see this everywhere. For example, when it comes to design and how you communicate with your marketplace, take a moment and pull up the Google homepage (meaning the one for the classic site). How cluttered is it? Not very.

Now think about that. From the Google home page, you can do lots of things with Google. You can check your Google mail, you can check your Google docs, you can find driving directions on Google Maps, etc. But at its core, what is Google all about? Exactly! Google is all about search. So what's the focus on that page? Search.

At the center is a big box for you to enter your search criteria in. And next to it is a big a search button. Everything else is minimized. It's clean and easy to figure out. Google is focused. They know what matters.

On the other hand, go ahead and pull up the Yahoo homepage. How cluttered is their page? Incredibly cluttered. Though they've finally made a few changes so that the search box is larger and more prominent (after years of obscurity), you can still read the news, get your horoscope, check the weather, shop, watch videos, play games, connect with your social media sites, check your stock portfolio, etc. all from the "comfort" of your Yahoo homepage. Is there any wonder that Google has come from behind and crushed Yahoo in the search world? Google is focused. Yahoo isn't. It's that simple!

Chet Holmes, in his book, The Ultimate Sales Machine, has a line that fits this concept so appropriately. He says,

> "Success isn't about doing 4,000 things; it's about doing a few things 4,000 times."

I love that line! Chet learned this concept of focusing on a few things from karate. He originally thought that to be great at karate he'd have to master lots and lots of intricate moves. But what he discovered was that karate was/is made up of a small number of moves that once mastered can be combined in a variety of different ways during a match. In other words, he didn't have to master 4,000 different moves to be successful at karate. He just needed to practice a few moves, over and over again, until they were ingrained and automatic.

However focus isn't just essential to karate. It's essential to your business as well. Verne Harnish, the CEO of Gazelles, Inc. made the following comment about Jack Welch at a seminar I attended of his.

> "In almost two decades of leadership, Jack Welch only had four 'number one' priorities."

Think about the power of that statement. For simplicity's sake, let's divide 20 years by four, which leaves us with four five-year increments. How many people do you know who could/can stay focused on one thing for, on average, five years? Probably not very many. Maybe there's a lesson in there. Maybe one of the reasons why GE did so well for the two decades that Jack was at its helm was precisely because he stayed focused and on one issue for a long period.

So what is it that keeps those of us who, "know better," from applying this simple principle about staying focused to our businesses? One of my answers, that's rarely discussed in owner and CEO circles, is what I call the problem of intelligence and education in leadership.

Note: I'm not opposed to either and am, in fact, a proponent of both. However, when it comes to leadership and business growth, intelligence and education are often overrated. Let me explain.

The more educated or intelligent a person is, the greater the probability that they prefer complexity over simplicity. If you've been through college or graduate school, you know that you were taught that highly intelligent people don't look for simple solutions. You were told that great questions don't have easy answers—and that black and white issues don't exist in reality.

In general, highly educated and intelligent people tend to look for shades of gray. They look for the nuances and deeper meanings. They tend to question the obvious and distrust what is accepted knowledge. And they have a clear disdain for simple answers like, "There are three things we do," when, in fact, they know that there are 476 things their company does.

But despite one's preference for complexity over simplicity, the key question for our discussion here is, "Does complexity power growth?" And the answer to that is, "No!" In fact there is a negative correlation between complexity and growth. The more complex an answer or solution or product or service or marketing campaign or communication—the less effective it is.

Now, this is not to say that intelligence and education are not important and valuable assets (they are). Rather, it's to say that left unchecked, they can be impediments to growth. Why? Because in order for an organization or business to grow faster, everything has to become simpler and more focused—and the leader at the top has to be willing to delegate and trust those whom they delegate to—without knowing all the details.

This is especially true the larger an organization gets. For example, when a business has only a few employees, the leader is able to touch base with his or her employees daily. Plans can be added to and adjusted daily. And the plans themselves can even be a little more complicated because, typically, the leader is onsite to answer any questions and to help assist in the implementation of the plans.

However, once a business or organization gets past a handful of employees, usually around eight or nine, everything changes. And by the time a business hits 40 or 50 employees, the "world" has changed. At this point, most employees have little to no interaction with the owner/CEO any more. The organization has layers of management. And it has systems and processes in place that can't be changed overnight.

At this point, most fast growth leaders figure out that they have to simplify everything in their business if they want to keep their business moving forward at a quickened pace. Why? Because they understand that no one can rally 25 or 50 or 150+ people around a twenty or fifty page plan. They understand that they can't meet with everyone one-on-one any longer. Nor, can they oversee everything. Therefore, once they pass the "two layers" point (where everyone no longer reports to them), fast growth leaders realize they need to simplify everything and reduce what the company is focused on down to one to three (a maximum of five) things they're going to focus their company on over the next twelve months.

In fact, Jeffery Immelt, who succeeded Jack Welch at GE, nailed this concept perfectly when he said,

> *"Every leader needs to clearly explain the top three things the organization is working on. If you can't then you're not leading well."*

So, what are your top three? Can you list them off the top of your head? Better yet, can everyone on your top team list them? How about the rest of your employees? Could they recreate the exact same list that you just enumerated in your head?

Hopefully, as you've been reading through this chapter, you've begun to think about a number of different areas in your business (or organization) where you need to create more focus so you can break through your plateau and build a bigger, better, faster and more profitable business (or organization). If not, here are a few suggestions to help you figure out what you should focus more on.

1. **Focus your target market more**

   No company or organization can be all things for all people. So, who should you focus on? Has "scope creep" slowly caused you to lose focus? Are you focused on too large of a market segment? Are you focusing on the right market? Can you niche down in your current market? Etc.

   The more focused and clearer you are on who your target market is (young mothers between the ages of 25-34 with two children under five at home in suburban areas around major cities in the Northeast who have a median household income of between $100K and $250K), the more powerful and productive your marketing will be to that target market.

2. **Focus your products and services more**

In a later chapter, we'll discuss adding new products and services to your product mix, but for now, let's just assume that the first problem you need to address is having too many products and/or services, not too few.

Note: This same problem is true for large companies as well. For example when Steve Jobs came back to Apple in the late 90's, one of his first acts as CEO was to cut their product line down to four products. Think about that. Steve cut whole product lines (with millions of dollars of revenue attached to them) just so he could create a more focused Apple that could do a few things really well. Then once they did those four things incredibly well, they began to strategically add new products and services — but only after they did some serious cutting first.

3. **Focus your strategic plans/goals/initiatives more**

Hopefully, as you've been reading this chapter, you've been thinking, "We're trying to do too much!" And you're probably right. Whenever I'm helping a business (or organization) create a strategic plan, I limit them to a maximum of five key initiatives. Why? Because it creates focus. Anything over five gets forgotten (and if you were to ask me personally, I'd tell you that five is too many). Most organizations get more done by focusing on a few key initiatives (three to five) than by trying to accomplish ten or more of them.

4. **Focus your time more**

You are a limited resource. If you're trying to do too many things or allow yourself to be pulled in too many different directions, you're killing your productivity. So my encouragement would be that you get very clear on your priorities and then stick with them. "Focus. Focus. Focus," should be one of your mantras.

5. **Focus your messaging more**

The key to all great marketing is learning to think like a customer. Customers (just like you) are busy and overwhelmed. They don't want complexity. They want simplicity. Once you remember that, you'll want to narrow down your messages in order to ensure that you're consistently communicating a simple easy-to-understand and remember message.

For example, your prospects don't need to know everything about your product and/or service. They only need to know enough to let them know that you have the solution for the problem or issue they're dealing with—that's it. In fact, a fun exercise to do is to go through your current website or marketing materials and, thinking like a customer, cut out everything that doesn't speak to their self-interest. Keep cutting it down until it's razor thin and focused. In essence, all you really need is, "Here's what you want and here's what we deliver to ensure that want is fulfilled (or your problem is solved)." Everything else is irrelevant.

6. **Focus your vision casting and internal messaging more**

We'll come back to this in driver #9, but one of the most important functions/roles you play in your business is that of chief vision caster. As such, you have to cast vision frequently—but it needs to be focused and on message. So often when I hear owners and CEOs try to cast vision, they're all over the place. This week it's this. Next week it's that. But a vision that's about everything is really a vision about nothing. So make sure your vision casting is very focused (and that you stay on message).

What most leaders forget is that vision leaks. Within 24-48 hours, most people have forgotten what they heard—which is why it's so important to have a focused message and say it over an over again (albeit with different stories and illustrations). As I say repeatedly to my clients, "Trust me, you can't cast vision too much!" If you want to keep everyone focused and aligned, you have to cast vision for whatever you're focused on — every day of every week.

So, if you'd like to break through your current plateau and get back on a growth curve, here are a few more ideas about how you can create more focus in your business (or organization).

1. **Use playoffs (i.e. use brackets) to get clarity on what you need to focus on.**

   Most organizations have more ideas than they can execute — yet they don't want to give up on any of their ideas because, well, they're all great ideas. So, how can you break through that list when you're at an impasse? One idea is to use brackets.

   For example, whenever I'm working with a business, I almost always end up doing some brainstorming with them, which means we always have more ideas than they can use. After some quick voting, there are usually a handful of ideas that rise to the top. However, no one can implement ten or fifteen "great ideas." So to help them select their top idea, I have them create a playoff chart, just like you see in a sports tournament.

   I have them vote on idea A vs. B. Let's say B wins. I then have them vote on idea C vs. D. Let's say C wins. Then I have them vote on idea B vs. C. Let's say C wins. C is the idea to focus on. You don't have to evaluate idea A vs. C or D vs. A because if the idea couldn't win earlier, it won't win later (unlike in sports). This simple tool is an incredibly powerful focusing tool!

2. **Engage your top team in defining what to focus on**

   Another common problem among small and medium-sized businesses is that their owners and/or CEOs often like to make all of the major decisions, which in and of itself is a bad decision. Why? Because people own what they help create. So if you want your top team to execute well, you want them to be involved in the process of choosing which ideas they're going to focus on.

   When I suggest this idea, a lot of owners push back and say, "But, what if they don't want to do what I want to do?" Hello, if you can't persuade your team that your idea is the best idea, then you've got another problem. But, that aside, it just might turn out that your idea might not be the best idea (I know, shocker). Believe it or not, someone on your team may have a better idea — which means that there's really very little downside to engaging your top team in the process of selecting your top three to five focused initiatives. Even better, there is a very huge upside for doing so — especially when it comes to creating accountability (which is my next thought)

3. **Create measurements and accountabilities around your focused objectives.**

As you know, what gets measured, gets done. If your staff members know that they're going to be held accountable and that that accountability is measurable, you're going to get more traction and execution than if it's generic and unquantifiable.

For example, let's say your team agrees that one of your problems is that you're out of touch with your customers. So you want to get back in touch with your customers' needs, wants and desires. Everyone agrees. That's good, but you and I know nothing is going to happen. At the next staff meeting when you ask, "How did it go?" you'll get silence.

But what if you were to go the next step at the end of your next meeting and you created some accountability. "Each of us agrees that we'll talk with at least five different customers each week for the next four weeks, correct?" That's better, but it still probably won't happen (other than a few random contacts). No, what will make that focused idea a reality is when you create a measurement that's reported. "And each week during staff meeting, we'll each take five minutes to share who we met with and what we learned from those customer interactions."

Bottom line, if you want to break through your plateau and once again lead a fast growth business, you've got to employ the driver of focus throughout your organization. You need to focus your priorities and plans. You need to focus your vision casting. You need to focus where you're going to invest your time. You need to focus your product line. You need to focus your strategic initiatives. You need to focus your marketing. Basically, at every level and in everything, you've got to create focus on a few key things, not a thousand things, if you want to get back on that growth curve!

Applying Driver #4: Focus

1. On a scale of 1-10 (high) how would you rate your ability to focus everyone on just a few key priorities? _____

2. What would you say are the top three priorities for your business (or organization) this year — that would help it break through your plateau and get it back on a growth curve?

3. What percentage of your people could write down on a piece of paper today the exact three priorities you just wrote down? _____

4. Why do you think you personally struggle with the subject of focus?

5. How do you think that's affected your company?

6. How do you think your own desire for complexity and new ideas has affected your organization?

7. What in your business needs more focus?

8. In light of your answers, what can you do to create more focus?

9. Where do you need to start?

10. What would you say is your major takeaway from this chapter?

11. What can you do within the next week to create more focus for your business (or organization)?

"We must all suffer from one of two pains: the pain of discipline or the pain of regret. The difference is discipline weighs ounces while regret weighs tons."

Jim Rohn, famous motivational speaker and successful businessman

Chapter 5
"Make Execution One of Your Core Competencies"

Driver #5: Discipline

If you were given the choice between two books to read, one of which was entitled, "Accelerated Growth Strategies: How to Double Your Business in Half the Time," and the other, "Discipline: The Five Practices You Must Engage in Every Day if You Want to Get Stuff Done," which would you choose?

If you're like most people, you'd gladly choose the former and pass on the later. Why? Because the idea of talking about discipline/execution sounds about as much fun as having a colonoscopy. Let's be honest, there's nothing fun, exciting or sexy about the idea or concept of discipline.

Yet, I would argue that the lack of consistent application of this driver is one of the main reasons why so many businesses and organizations hit plateaus—and can't seem to break through them. Ideas are great (and apart from them a business is destined to be a commodity). However, those ideas are meaningless if there's no consistent discipline to follow through and execute on them.

If you don't believe me, take a moment and think back through the past twelve months of your business (or organization). How many ideas have you and your team come up with that you haven't executed? My guess is that it's a rather large number. And of the ideas you have executed, how many of them have you stayed on top of — week after week, month after month? Again, chances are it's a small number.

Which explains a lot, doesn't it? The fact that so few small and medium-sized businesses are great at creating a culture of discipline and execution explains why so many of them are stuck on a plateau. They're good at coming up with ideas (or hearing or reading about ideas from other businesses). They'll write them down in a plan. But then, because they don't have the discipline (i.e. the bulldog tenacity) to execute and stay on task for a long period of time, they rarely complete those ideas.

On the other hand, successful growth-oriented business leaders are masters of this key business driver of disciple. Thomas Edison, who's inventive output was extraordinary, clearly understood this. In fact, he once made the following statement about discipline (which he refers to as, "stick-to-it-iveness").

> *"The three great essentials to achieve anything worthwhile are, first, hard work; second, stick-to-it-iveness; third, common sense."*

Now, if discipline/stick-to-it-iveness/execution/bulldog tenacity/pigheaded persistence is so critical to breaking through a plateau and starting a new growth cycle, why it is that so few entrepreneurial leaders use it? Why is it that so few owners and entrepreneurs of small businesses are great at executing with discipline?

My four top reasons are:

1. **By nature, entrepreneurial leaders tend to be idea people, not implementation people**.

   They like to create, start, innovate, change, and destroy. So, the whole idea/practice of discipline isn't part of their make up. They like to be on the front-side of an idea, not the back end. They like to get things started, but, in general, they don't like to be involved in finishing up a project.

2. **Entrepreneurial leaders tend to get bored rather easily.**

Once an idea is hatched, they want to move on to discover the next egg they can hatch. The idea of staying on top of an idea for any length of time until it's inculcated and part of the company culture, is about as exciting as watching paint dry to an entrepreneurial leader.

3. **Entrepreneurial leaders tend to tolerate poor performance way too long**

In general, entrepreneurial leaders don't like to hold people accountable. This behavior is caused by a number of factors, but the main one is that entrepreneurial leaders are often driven by fear — fear of the work that won't get done while they're looking for a new person, or fear of how others will respond to the firing, or fear of rejection, or fear of what letting someone go will do to their relationship, or fear of being held accountable themselves, etc. So, instead of confronting their fears, most owners and entrepreneurs tend to hold on to poor performers way too long.

4. **Entrepreneurial leaders get too wrapped up in their own work and don't want to spend their time managing other people.**

Unfortunately, that is not an option. As a leader, managing your people is you job. Remember, a leader is someone who produces results through other people. It's not your work that matters, but the work that your people get done that matters. In other words, a lot of ideas don't get executed in an organization because the leader of that business or organization doesn't realize that one of their jobs is to ensure that discipline/execution takes place. While a lot of entrepreneurial leaders like the idea of hiring someone to take care of making sure their staff gets their work done — this is not something that can be delegated away. Discipline always flows from the top down.

5. **Entrepreneurial leaders don't like to be held accountable themselves**

As I discuss at length in my course on "Personality Type Leadership: How to Lead People Who Don't Think, Act, and Feel Like You," (www.PersonalityTypeLeadership.com), one of the classic mistakes that most leaders make is that they tend to lead others the way they like to be led. The problem with that mindset is that most people aren't like us. Nor is what we need, always what they need.

So, in this case, if a leader doesn't like to be held accountable, what will they, in general, do? Exactly! They won't hold others accountable — even if they intellectually know that they ought to hold their own people accountable for results.

Looking at your own life, which of the above five reasons best suits you? Why?

Once you've wrestled with that, the next question is, "So, what's the solution?" How can you turn this around so that you and your business have a more disciplined and execution-oriented culture so that what you say you're going to do and what you actually get done are in harmony?

Well, to help you get started, here are a few ideas for how you can go about doing that.

1. **When you announce a plan or initiative, mentally commit to riding it through until it's accomplished.**

   While the idea of simply creating ideas and then passing them off to others is a pleasurable thought to most entrepreneurial leaders, it's a terrible leadership/management practice. A better idea is to make a commitment that when you introduce an idea, you need to mentally commit to it for MONTHS, not days or weeks. Change is almost always more difficult than we like to think. And unless the person (or people) at the top of an organization (or department) are committed to staying focused and disciplined until that change becomes a reality, chances are, nothing will happen.

2. **Make sure you summarize commitments at the end of each meeting with your people — and then review them at the beginning of the next meeting.**

   I watch this happen all the time. An executive team meets. They discuss. They make decisions. They leave without ever reviewing what decisions were made or what actions need to be taken or who's responsible for which actions. Instead, they assume that everyone knows what they're supposed to do between then and the next meeting. Even worse, at the next meeting no one checks to make sure that those who were assigned tasks actually did them — usually because the person leading the meeting didn't get their stuff done and/or can't remember who was assigned what. Either way, there's no accountability, which is why so many tasks don't get done.

In order to turn that around, what I recommend to all my clients is that they stop whatever meetings they're leading five to ten minutes early (depending on the length of the meeting) and then run back through all the decisions that were made (Note: If you're not making decisions at your meetings, then that's another problem). As you review each decision, make sure everyone is clear on what was decided, who is responsible, and what they should bring back to the group at the next meeting. Also, make sure notes and assignments are distributed shortly after the meeting.

Then, and this is just as vital, you need to start your next meeting by reviewing the assignments from the last meeting. At first you'll probably find some resistance and a lot of "dropped balls", but it won't take long until your people realize you're serious about this discipline/execution thing. Most people hate to be called out in a group where they have to say, "Sorry, I didn't get anything done on that."

If you simply start doing these two things, wrapping up meetings by reviewing assignments and decisions made and then start your next meeting (with that same group of people) by making sure their assignments were completed, you'll automatically begin creating a more disciplined culture.

3. **Make execution easy**.

While project management is helpful and necessary (and something your team will hopefully embrace at some point in the future), if your team isn't great at execution, chances are detailed project management plans won't help as much as you might like to think.

For poor executors, detailed plans with diagrams, graphs, milestones, pert charts and Gantt charts, tend to get in the way and cause them to become bogged down in minutia. If that's the case for your team—don't let that happen. Instead, make execution easy by continually talking about the 5W's and 1H (who, what, when, where, why and how).

For example, let's say your team is going to organize a conference and you've assigned Sally to find the location (which is a very generic task and wide open to interpretation and misunderstanding, which might hinder some people from completing it).

So, before your meeting is over. Walk up to a whiteboard and create a table with the 5Ws and 1H (Note: because of the orientation of this book, I'm filling them in as a list vs. a table). Then simply fill in the table as a team, giving as much detail as is necessary to successfully complete the task.

- **What**: Research locations for our upcoming users conference with an anticipated attendance of 250 people. Note: Isn't that a lot clearer than, "Find a location"?
- **Who:** Sally
- **When:** By next Wednesday's staff meeting
- **Where:** Within a 30 minute drive of our offices
- **Why:** The art department can't create the direct mail pieces until we nail down a location and the mail pieces need to be in the mail by September 7th.
- **How:** Call Jenny over at Conference Locations Services and ask her to provide you with her top three recommendations by next Tuesday.

Note: It's that "How" question that's often left out and that's a huge problem. Why? Because chances are, in a small business, the way you think and the way your people think is probably radically different. In other words, you may be thinking this task is a five-minute conversation, (Just call Jenny over at Conference Locations Services), whereas Sally is probably thinking, "Oh great! My boss wants me to do all this research (web research, make a bunch of calls, go make a bunch of site visits, etc.) on top of my already busy schedule. There's no way I can get this done by next week." So while you're thinking, "This is an easy five minute assignment," Sally's ticked and thinking, "This is like a two day job. Ugh!"

I can't over-emphasize how important this practice is. It's so simple. And yet it's so powerful. Even better, once you start doing this regularly, you'll be amazed at how often it clears up misunderstandings and enhances execution — which are both essential if you want to get back on a double-digit growth curve.

4.   **Make sure you model discipline in your own life.**

As you've probably noticed, I'm a huge fan of the principle, "People do what people see." If they see you leaving a meeting and executing an idea right away, they'll get the idea that execution is what "we," as a company do. But if you don't, they'll get the idea that execution doesn't really matter around here.

Likewise, if you create a plan and week-by-week hold yourself accountable for the plan, they'll get the idea that discipline matters. If you don't, they'll notice that as well.

In other words, if you model consistency — consistency is what you'll get. However, if you have a habit of saying you'll get something done, and then don't — you'll also get that kind of culture back. We always get what we model. So, if you don't like what you see out there, make sure you check your own modeling. If you want discipline and consistent execution, then you have to make sure that you're modeling discipline day in and day out. Or to put it another way, "Discipline is as discipline does."

5.   **Ensure that evaluation is a part of your culture.**

Virtually, "everyone knows," they should engage in more regular evaluation. The problem, of course, is that very few do. I get to watch this in business after business all the time. Whenever I ask, "What was the last thing you evaluated as a team?" there's almost always an awkward moment of silence. Finally someone says, "It's been awhile." Note: The same thing happens whenever I ask a solopreneur the same question.

Why is that? I think the main reason is that most of us are so busy trying to get everything done that we haven't completed, that the idea of taking time to evaluate what we've already completed, just doesn't seem to make sense.

However, as you saw in the chapter on optimization, not taking the time to evaluate and optimize, is an incredibly costly decision. So, my recommendation to you is that you make evaluation an easy process that's integrated into every project, process and/or event.

In fact, what I recommend is that you train your people to ask five very simple and yet critical questions after every project, process/system design, marketing campaign, event/conference, etc. The military calls them After Action Reviews, I prefer to call them After Action Optimization Reviews (because of question #4). Note: You can download a template form with these five questions already laid out for you at http://wiredtogrow.com/free/free-tools-and-helps/

The five questions you should be continually asking after every event, project, process, campaign, etc. are:

1. **What worked?**
2. **What didn't?**
3. **What did I/we learn**? Note: Most never ask this question, yet it's critical to ask.
4. **What could I/we test and do differently next time to get a better result?** Note: This is the key question if you want to optimize (and you should ☺).
5. **What will we do differently next time?**

Short, simple and business changing! Ask these five questions all the time about everything.

So, if you'd like to help your business or organization break through its current plateau, make sure you work on raising the level of discipline and execution in your business. And from now on, don't just announce an idea, ride it for a long time until it becomes a part of what you do. Change is never easy. But with discipline, modeled from you, it becomes infinitely easier.

Application Driver #5: Discipline

1. On a scale of 1-10 (high), how would you evaluate your company's discipline/execution culture? _____

2. On a scale of 1-10 (high), how would you rate your own discipline — your ability to stay on task and get things done on time? _____

3. What do you think hinders YOU from being more disciplined?

4. How do you think you, personally, hinder your business' (or organization's) ability to execute?

5. What do you think hinders your company from being disciplined and executing faster?

6. What do you think would help create a better culture of execution in your business or organization?

7. Create a 5W's and 1H grid for a current project with your team at your next team meeting.

8. Download the After Action (Optimization) Review and use it at least once this week.

9. What would you say is your major takeaway from this chapter?

10. What is one thing you can do this week to improve your team's discipline and ability to execute better?

Chapter 6
"Clearly Define Why You're Different"

Driver #6: Differentiation

Why do you buy what you buy from where you buy it? For example, why do you buy from the grocery store that you buy from vs. any other grocery store? Or why do you buy your clothes at the clothing store you buy from vs. any other clothing store? Or why do you choose to stay at the hotel chain that you normally stay at when traveling vs. any of the other hotels you could choose from (chain or non-chain)?

In other words, there are certain reasons why you and I choose one provider of a product or service over every other option in that specific market space. For example, going back to the grocery store market, if given the choice, would you choose Whole Foods or Giant? Costco or Safeway? A local Asian market or Wegmans? If given the choice, which would you choose?

More importantly, why would you choose one over the other? Is price your primary determinant? Or do you care more about ambiance? Does the look and feel of a store matter to you? Does having a large selection matter? Or do you look for a store that carries certain brands that you like? How about customer service? Does it matter if the employees are happy, smiling, helpful, knowledgeable and fast? Or is that all irrelevant to you (and you just want cheap)?

Whether it's a conscious process or not, you (and every other consumer) use some kind of decision process/grid/filter to determine which provider you (or they) are going to use to meet that need or want in your life (or theirs). The company or vendor that best matches your criteria is said to have a competitive advantage over all of the other vendors you could have chosen. There is something different about them that causes you to say, on a consistent basis, "I choose this vendor as the best option to meet my need/want."

On the other hand, if all of the vendors seem similar — or if all of their offers appear to be interchangeable, then there's no real competitive advantage or differentiation, which means that you are, in Ken Blanchard's words, "A revolt waiting to happen," meaning that the next time you have to choose a vendor, you'll try someone else out (and chances are, price will become a dominant force in your decision criteria — something no vendor really wants).

Now, if you choose with whom you're going to do business on the basis of differentiation/competitive advantage, doesn't it stand to reason that your potential customers are probably using that exact same process to decide if they should buy from you and your business? Absolutely!

So, if I were to ask you, "Why should anyone buy from you (and your company) versus any other vendor in your market space?" what would you say? I've asked this question of a ton of owners, CEOs, and executive teams over the years and rarely have any of them had a good answer.

Most respond with, "That's a great question." While the rest respond with some kind of generic answer. See if you can relate to any of the following.

- "Our products (or services) are better." Or, "We have the best _____"
- "Our customer service is better."
- "Our prices are lower (or our fees or loan rates are lower)"
- "We offer the best value for your money"
- "We have the best online …"
- "We have the best people in our industry"
- "Our people are more friendly"
- "We put your interests before our own"

Now, as you were reading through that list, how many of those sounded like real differentiators or competitive advantages? None! Why? Because generic answers mean nothing. When "everyone" is saying the same thing, it means that "no one" is saying anything.

"Yeah, but our products really are better!" Who cares? Ho hum. If you really believe your products (or services) are better — then prove it. Don't just say it — give us some proof and then you'll establish true differentiation.

For example, when I originally wrote this chapter, Singapore Airlines had a series of ads it ran in several business magazines that started with the following statement, "Thank you for making us the World's Most Awarded Airline." The ad then listed five magazines to back that up.

- From Conde Nast Traveler, "*Reader's Choice Award, Top International Airline (21 out of 22 years)."*
- From Travel + Leisure, "*World's Best Award, World's Best International Airline (14 out of 14 years)."*
- From Global Traveler, "*GT Tested Award, Best Airline in the World (6 out of 6 years)."*
- From Executive Travel, "*Leading Edge Award, Best International Airline (4 out of 4 years)."*
- And from Business Traveler, "*Best in Business Travel Award, Best Airline in the World (21 out of 22 years)."*

Now, as you read through that list, what did you think about Singapore Airlines? Chances are you thought, "They must be the best airline in the world!" Note: Not because they said it they were, but because others said they were — which then makes us believe that it's more likely to be true. Those reviews are a competitive advantage. What other airline could offer the same proof? American? United? Continental? Delta? US Air? Southwest?

You see, once you begin to look at your business through the set of differentiation lenses, you begin to realize that fast growth companies have always been great at doing this. For example, GEICO has been on a growth spurt for years using its slogan, "15 minutes can save you 15% or more on your car insurance." Wal-Mart grew with its slogan, "Every day low prices." Dominos Pizza grew with its differentiator (when it took the nation by storm) of, "Fresh, hot pizza delivered to your door in 30 minutes or it's free." A few years ago, Southwest created a new differentiator, "Your bags fly free," which only became a differentiator when the other major airlines decided to charge for luggage (in other words, it wasn't a differentiator before that happened because no one was charging for bags at the time).

That said, I don't want you to get the idea that competitive advantages are about slogans — because they're not. For example, Apple's differentiator isn't a tagline, it's their ability to innovate and make cool, beautifully designed and easy-to-use devices that create an almost magical experience for their customers. Or 1-800-Got-Junk's competitive advantage isn't a slogan, but rather their clean trucks and friendly uniformed "garbage collectors" (who are called "Customer Service Truck Team Members") who even sweep up after the job is done.

Now, the reason why this conversation is so important to helping you get your business or organization up off a plateau is because this is where plateaued companies get stuck. When prospects can't observe a real discernable difference between you and the other options in your market space — you're in trouble. Why? Because then you're perceived to be nothing more than a commodity.

Note: this isn't meant to be harsh, it's meant to be a reality check. At the end of the day, it doesn't matter what you or I think about your company — it only matters what your customers and potential customers think. And how owners and prospects think is usually radically different.

For example, let's say you run a Chinese restaurant. In your mind, you probably think that your restaurant is very different from every other Chinese restaurant — but remember, what you think is irrelevant. What matters is what your potential customers think. And what do they think? Based on the conversations I've had, most people think that a Chinese restaurant is a Chinese restaurant is a Chinese restaurant. In other words, there's no differentiation. To most people, a Chinese restaurant is a commodity and therefore interchangeable with every other Chinese restaurant. Unless there's something that differentiates that Chinese restaurant — and that differentiation is widely known — it's stuck in the commodity zone.

Now, not to be hard on Chinese restaurants, no business or organization is exempt from this conversation. Commoditization happens everywhere, regardless of whether we're talking about churches or credit unions, hospitals or shoe stores, health clubs or arts centers, dental offices or law firms. Whenever there's no real discernable difference between different options in a market, commoditization takes over—which is one of the main reasons why so many plateaued companies stay plateaued. There's no clear compelling reason why someone should choose that business (or organization) over every other option in that market

So if you'd like to break through your plateau and get back on a growth curve, you're going to want to learn how to create truly compelling competitive advantages for your business (or organization).

How do you do that? Well, here are a few ideas to help you get started on this journey toward creating a series of truly compelling competitive advantages that will position you as being the obvious provider of choice in your market.

1. **Think in terms of competitive advantages, not "a" competitive advantage**

   When creating your competitive advantages, you don't want to think of creating just one advantage—you want to think of creating at least three—and the more the merrier. For example, Southwest isn't just about low fares. And it's not just about bags flying free. It's also about no hubs (i.e. you get direct flights without layovers). It's about second tier cities. It's about no-assigned seats. It's about fun (and wacky airline attendants who crack jokes). And it's about a phenomenal record of leaving and arriving on time. In other words, it's not just one thing that differentiates Southwest from other carriers. It's lots of things. You want the same.

   So, don't just think of coming up with only one competitive advantage. Think lots of advantages.

2. **Revisit your competitive advantages often**

   One of the more common mistakes that businesses (and organizations) make about competitive advantages is that they think of coming up with a list of advantages—and then run with that list of advantages for years!

   However, defining your competitive advantages shouldn't be a one-time strategic exercise. It should be an ongoing, continual practice. In fact, one of my favorite quotes about competitive advantages comes from David Neeleman, when he used to be the CEO of Jet Blue, and was asked by Jaynie Smith about how often he and his team reviewed their competitive advantages. Neelman said,

"We revisit our competitive advantages EVERY WEEK when we ask ourselves,

- *What do we do better than them?*
- *What do they do better than us?*
- *How can we do that better than them?"*

The reason why you need to do this regularly is because your competitors aren't sitting idly by. They're making moves in your market space. They're sending messages out to your prospects. They're offering similar products and services to your potential customers. Which means that if you're not constantly monitoring what they're doing and what messages they're sending out—what was a competitive advantage when you originally came up with it, may no longer be one.

Or, to put it another way, differentiation isn't a one-time off-site exercise. It's a constant ongoing process that never ends!

3. **Quantify your competitive advantages**

Anytime you can quantify a competitive advantage the more powerful it is. For example, for several years, Zyrtec ran an ad in print and through various media stating that Zyrtec worked, "Two hours faster than Claritin." Now, whether that is or was true, is irrelevant. In fact, in my family, Claritin works for me, Zyrtec works for my wife, Allegra works for one of my daughters and Claritin D for my other daughter.

The point is not whether or not the statement is true, but rather that, "Two hours faster!" was a powerful differentiator. If Zytec had simply said, "Works faster than Claritin," do you think that would have moved the market? No way. Everyone knows you can lie with statistics. So, what does "works faster" mean? A second faster? A minute faster? Those would all be, by definition, faster. But two hours faster? Now, that's a differentiator. Even better, it caused many of us who are Claritin takers to think less of our product, "I didn't know it took so long for my allergy meds to work. Claritin must not be as good as I thought!"

Note: This is also a compelling reason why you need to test and measure the results of your products and/or services. Why? Because the right data can create truly compelling competitive advantages – if you can prove that your product or service is demonstrably better than the other options.

Now, when it comes to actually defining what your competitive advantages should be, you have a lot of options to choose from. In fact, I've identified well over 70 different types of typical competitive advantages you can choose from (but don't worry I won't bore you with all of them). Instead, I'm just going to share with you the nine major categories of competitive advantages, along with a few quick examples of each so you can get a better grasp of the different kinds of competitive advantages you can choose from to differentiate your business.

1. **Convenience advantages.**

    For example, your location could be a competitive advantage ("We're the only Japanese steak house on the east side of the city."). The number of locations you have could be your differentiator ("We have 27 branches around our county"). Your hours of operation could be a differentiator ("We're the only doctors' office open seven days a week (from 7:00 a.m.-8:00 p.m. M-F and 9:00 a.m. – 3:00 p.m. on Saturday and Sunday"). In other words, anything that makes it easy and convenient for a prospect or customer to do business with you and/or get a solution to their problem or need could be a significant differentiator for your business.

    So how can you make your business more convenient?

2. **Expertise advantages**

    When it comes to expertise, your level of education could be a differentiator ("80% of our researchers have Ph.Ds."). Your ratings could be a differentiator ("J.D. Power has rated us #1 in our category for the past five years."). If you've published a book or important article/report, that could be a differentiator

("Author of the NY Times Best-selling book ...). Or your experience could be your differentiator. Taking a riff on McDonald's "Billions of burgers served" ("We've completed over 1,500 successful rotator cuff surgeries."). All of these would be examples of competitive advantages surrounded by the idea that you possess some kind of expertise that others don't.

So do you have any expertise advantages you can market?

3. **Results advantages**

Sometimes, what can set you business apart from every other business in your market space is the results you generate. These could be the results that your clients receive ("Our typical clients reduce their administrative costs by 37%"). Or your advantage could be based on your retention rate ("97% of our customers use us for additional projects"). Or your results advantage would be related to your safety record ("We're the safest investment company in our industry with zero claims filed against us"). In other words, if you have any results that set you apart from your competitors, you can use them in your marketing to differentiate you from them.

So do you have any stellar results that could differentiate you?

4. **Selection advantages**

Selection advantages are all about the options — the choices you present to your market space. For example, the product line you offer (from a specific vendor) could be a differentiator ("We're the exclusive retailer in our county for XYZ designer."). The quantity of your selection could be your differentiator (Can you say, "Superstore? Or Amazon? Or 500,000 apps?"). The quality of your selection could be your differentiator ("We only use 100% _____ from _____"). One of my favorite selection advantages to use is the package or bundle of services differentiator. Why? Because you can combine things no one else offers as a bundle and then give it its own name, which, by definition, means it's unique/different (i.e. "Home of the Johnson Ultimate Power Pack Plus").

So what kinds of selection options could make your business the obvious choice in your market?

5. **Design advantages**

    This fifth category of competitive advantages is based on how
    the product or service is designed (i.e. the look and feel of
    something). For example, you could differentiate your product
    on the basis of color ("We offer this in six different colors" – a
    strategy that clearly worked for the original iMac. Note: Before
    you dismiss color, back in the 90's, who would have thought
    that color would move someone to buy a computer?).

    Cleanliness could be your differentiator ("We have sparkling
    clean bathrooms you can use while your child plays soccer on
    our outdoor fields"). Innovation could be a design differentiator
    (Again, think, "Apple!"). Ease of use could also be your
    differentiator ("We use universal design principles" -- think,
    OXO kitchen appliances and hand tools). In other words, the
    way you design your product or service can, in fact, cause
    certain people to buy from you – which is what makes design
    such an important differentiator.

    So are there any design advantages you could market?

6. **Financial advantages**

    Whenever you can lift up a differentiator that appeals to
    someone's financial interests--that could clearly move a
    prospect to choose you. For example, being the high-priced
    option in your market could be your differentiator ("We're the
    Rolls Royce of ..."). Similarly, you could be the low-priced
    option in your market ("We're the Wal-Mart of ..."). Or you
    could offer a fixed price option that could become your
    differentiator ("Home of the $999 divorce package").

    Or, depending on your market, coming in on or under budget
    could be a huge differentiator ("98% of our projects come in on
    time and under budget."). And, as always, savings could be a
    huge differentiator ("Our customers save, on average,
    $3,500/year when they switch to us."). In other words,
    whenever you can create an advantage over your competitors
    using money, you can create a financial advantage worth
    marketing.

    So what financial advantages could differentiate your offerings?

7. **Experience advantages**

Another way you can create a competitive advantage over the other vendors in your market is by appealing to the experience they have with you. For example, you could create your differentiator around the customer experience ("You'll be greeted at the airport in a limo with a glass of champagne awaiting you"). You could differentiate based on customer support ("All support tickets are responded to within five minutes or less"). Or you could differentiate based on your return policy ("We have a no-questions asked return policy — and we pay for the return shipping"). Or you could differentiate on the Southwest theme of fun in your market. In other words, anything you do that differentiates the kind of experience a customer will have with you over your competitors can become your experience competitive advantage.

So is there anything about the experience your customers have with your business that could make you the obvious choice?

8. **Celebrity advantages**

As you're hopefully beginning to realize, the list of possible advantages is almost endless. For example, celebrities can be a huge advantage/differentiator. In fact, you don't have to look much further than George Foreman to know this. How many George Foreman Grills do you think he sold? Maybe you could hire a celebrity and create an advantage none of your competitors can.

In addition, celebrity doesn't have to always be a paid endorsement. For example, a local tea company here in Maryland, Honest Tea, could easily say, "We're President Obama's favorite tea." Or, maybe you have a little celebrity yourself. For example, if you've been on a local TV show or cable reality show you could differentiate yourself from everyone else in your market space ("As seen on HGTV").

Don't overlook celebrity as an option. There is a reason businesses pay celebrities good money to endorse their products. It works!

So could celebrity work for your business? If so, who?

9. Company advantages

Finally, the last major category of competitive advantages is based on your company. For example, your competitive advantage could be that you were the first to make something ("Home of the Original _____"). Or your differentiator could be the size of your market reach ("We have consultants in twelve major metro markets") or the size of your company itself ("We have over 100 licensed contractors in our county at your disposal"). In other words, whenever there is something unique about your company (as a company) that could make a difference to a prospect and cause them to say, "I want you!" that would be a company-oriented competitive advantage.

So is there anything unique about your company that could make you the obvious choice in your market?

Hopefully, now that we've gone through this list of the top nine categories of differentiators, you believe me when I say that there are plenty of ways you can differentiate your business or organization from your competitors. Even better, we've just scratched the surface on this subject and, hopefully, you already have several ideas swimming around in your head about how you could differentiate your business (or organization).

But before we leave this conversation on competitive advantages, here are a few more thoughts I'd like to pass along to you.

1. You really can't engage in creating real competitive advantages apart from doing two very important things.

One, getting to know your customers. And two, getting to know your competitors. Yes, I know there are some businesses that think that "worrying" about what your competitors are doing is irrelevant—but they're wrong (and moreover, they're not being honest). If you're offering a product or service to anyone, you need to think like them. And part of thinking like them is being aware of the options they believe are in front of them. In other words, while you may like to think that you're the only one who can satisfy someone's needs/wants, that's not how they're thinking (nor how you think about what you want outside of what your business offers).

So, make sure you study your customers and your competitors. Get to know them so well that you'll instinctively know what the right differentiators are for your market—based on what they want and your competitors either don't have or can't compete on.

2. **No differentiator is worth its salt unless it's marketed well.**

At the end of the day, who cares if you know what differentiates you—but your market doesn't. In other words, once you define what you believe your differentiators are, you need to market the heck out of those differentiators so that everyone in your market knows them. It never ceases to amaze me how many businesses will define their competitive advantages and then sit on them. Listen, you want your prospects and potential customers to be able to do what GEICO's prospects and potential customers can do—say, "GEICO. Oh yeah, they're the '15 minutes can save you 15% or more on your car insurance' people'."

Bottom line, if the people in your target market can't clearly state what your competitive advantages are, you don't have any.

However, that said, there is some good news for you. The vast majority of businesses are awash in the sea of sameness. They look, feel, smell, and taste just like every other vendor in their market—which is one of the main reasons why so many businesses are stuck on a plateau. They don't have a compelling marketing message that separates them out from everyone else. And if there's no compelling differentiation between two or more companies, then commoditization has taken over—and every business becomes a casualty of the price and convenience war.

Now, you might be thinking, "Where's the good news in that?" Well, the good news is that since so few businesses do this well, if you become great at creating and then communicating your competitive advantages, you can literally own your market.

So, if you want to break through your plateau and get back on a double-digit growth curve, you'll want to make sure that you and your top team regularly carve out time in your schedules to think about and establish market-moving differentiators!

Application Driver #6: Differentiation

1. On a scale of 1-10 (high), how would you rate your business on its ability to differentiate itself – and then communicate that differentiation to your target market? _____ Why?

2. Off the top of your head, how would you answer the question, "Why should anyone in our market choose to use our business vs. every other option in our market space?"

3. How many of your answers sound generic (or similar to what your competitors would say)?

4. What, do you think, are the greatest needs and wants of your target market?

5. What do your competitors do better than you?

6. What do you do better than them?

7. So what would you say are your top three competitive advantages? Remember to reflect back on the nine major categories.

8. Can you quantify any of those advantages? How?

9. What would you say is your major takeaway from this chapter?

10. What is one thing you can do this week to improve your business' ability to differentiate itself from your competition?

Chapter 7
"Stay on the Front Side of the S-Curve"

Driver #7: Addition

Do you happen to know how much of Apple's revenue comes from selling computers? Believe it or not, only 20% of their revenue comes from selling computers (about 6.5% comes from desktops and 13.9% from laptops—and that despite the growth of the Mac line by over 30%). Now, just image for a moment, that back in 1997 when Steve Jobs returned, Apple said, "We're a computer company and only a computer company. Nothing more. Nothing less." What would Apple have missed out on? You got it. Billions!!!!

The iPhone and iPad alone account for well over half of Apple's revenue (two revenue streams that didn't exist five years ago). In fact, in quarter two of 2011, Apple sold over $10.7B worth of iPhones, over $4.7B worth of iPads, over $3.6B worth of iPods and $1.43B in music for the quarter (none of which are "computers").

If you ever needed proof that this driver is critical to your growth, you need look no further than Apple. Once a computer company, Apple (which dropped the name "Computer" from their name several years ago) now derives most of its revenue from seven primary revenue streams (iPhone, iPad, iPod, Mac, iTunes, Software, and Peripherals). Unfortunately, most plateaued small businesses don't get this principle.

In fact, it's one of the reasons why so many small and medium-sized businesses get stalled or stuck on a plateau. Why? Because they keep riding something that once was successful for far too long. For example, it's not unusual for a small business to start out offering one primary product or service. And, based on the principle of focus we discussed a few chapters ago, they probably grew faster than their competitors who were trying to offer too many products and services.

But, now that they're closing in on, let's say the $1M mark, chances are they're starting to hit a plateau (Note: this is a normal and predictable plateau for most small businesses). Now, there are a whole host of reasons why this tends to occur. For example, it could be they're getting closer to market saturation; or more competitors have entered the market seeing how good this company is doing, or it customers are getting bored with this product or service. In fact, one of my more frequent sayings is, "Everything in life goes from remarkable to ordinary to death,"--meaning it no longer satisfies.

Regardless, the point here is that companies/businesses/ organizations/non-profits/associations/ churches etc. all get to a point where they have to add something to the mix in order to create the next growth curve. You can only ride a cash cow/strategy/tactic for so long until it no longer delivers like it used to.

Hopefully you remember the lifecycle of an idea graph that you learned years ago in school. If you do, then you'll remember that every idea, every product, every organization, every relationship, every service, every government, every policy, etc. goes through a predictable life cycle (also known as the S-curve).

In stage one, you have to work very hard to get an idea off the ground. It's about lots of effort and very minimal results. In stage two, it's nirvana. The idea hits its growth curve and life is good. At this stage you can't ever imagine it ending. But what everyone forgets is that stage three always comes after stage two. In stage three, all of those great growth gains slow down and eventually come to a halt. And in stage four, results go backwards until the idea dies a slow (or occasionally fast) death.

Now, it would be great if this life cycle didn't apply to you or me or our businesses — but it does. Every business, every product, every service, every idea goes through this same predictable life cycle. Are you depressed yet? Can I get an "Amen"?

Well, you don't need to be because the solution to this problem of the lifecycle of an idea is to avoid the problem of the S-Curve altogether. How? By learning to create a series of consecutive S-Curves.

In other words, when your current product or service (or marketing idea or customer service initiative etc.) is in the steep part of the growth curve going upwards (stage 2), right when you're finally feeling good about all that early work you did when you weren't seeing any results — that's when you need to start the next new thing (i.e. start a new growth curve so that when your current idea enters the plateau of stage three, your new idea is entering the fast growth part of the S-curve so that it counteracts the decline of results from your current idea).

If you were to pick two companies that are radically different on this point, I'd pick Dell vs. Apple. For example, when Dell first started picking up steam, it came up with a great model of compiling PCs in a highly efficient and cost effective way. And because they did so, they stormed the market. Unfortunately, they ran that model for way too long, which gave others time to catch up, copy their ideas and even create better ones-- and the result is that others have stolen a fair amount of market share away from Dell.

On the other hand, Apple is constantly inventing and reinventing itself. In fact, one of my favorite leadership moments occurred several years ago when Steve Jobs was giving his Apple keynote address, shortly after Apple had introduced the iPod mini. Steve stood on stage with all these graphs on slides showing how the iPod mini had taken the world by storm. He was talking about how the iPod mini had been (up to that moment) their most successful product launch ever, how they were making a lot of money, and how other companies were trying to copy the iPod mini etc. Then he said something I'll never forget.

"Which is why today we're killing the iPod mini ... (pregnant pause) ... and introducing the iPod nano."

As he said those words I thought, "Who else would do that?" Who else would kill a cash cow after just a few months on the market? Most businesses leaders I know wouldn't. They'd ride that cash cow for as long as possible (including yours truly). But what has made Apple the darling of the world is that they keep adding and changing, inventing and reinventing year after year.

Likewise, if you want to break through your plateau, you're going to need to do some inventing and reinventing of your own — Apple style. You're going to need to add some new things to your business that you haven't tried yet (and probably drop some old things that aren't delivering like they used to). And to help you get started on using this "addition" driver, let me suggest that you start looking at three key areas to begin adding in.

1. **You could add a new product and/or service**

    This may seem like the obvious add, but it's not. Far too many companies keep the same old product line/menu of options that "we've always had," year after year. But if you want to keep growth moving forward, you have to keep adding new options and new revenue streams to your mix.

    For example, let's say you're a chiropractor and most of your money comes from doing adjustments. The key question would be, "What other products or services would be LOGICAL extensions of a chiropractic practice?" Well, message therapy would be one. As would nutritional supplements or physical therapy or personal training or weight management/food consultations, etc. In other words, just by adding new products and/or services, you could significantly increase your total revenues.

    Of course, the big question is, which one (or ones) should you choose? Well, as every consultant on the planet knows the correct answer is, "That depends!" Having said that, let me offer you five quick guidelines/questions to help you make a solid choice.

    a. **"What would be a logical extension of what we're currently offering?"**

        In other words, what would make sense to your customers? Offering discount theater tickets or selling tax software for a chiropractic office wouldn't quite fit this logical extension guideline.

    b. **"Is it profitable?" "And, if so, "Does the margin justify the time and effort?"**

        Again, these would seem to be two rather obvious questions, but they're not. And not just because they aren't often asked, but because a high percentage of business leaders don't know their numbers. I'm continually shocked by how many business owners don't know their cost of goods sold. They don't know their fixed costs vs. their variable costs. Or they don't know what their profit margins or profit margins per product/service are.

Now, if a leader doesn't know their numbers, then there's no way they're going to ask and answer the profit and margin questions above. Which is why you'll often see companies on a plateau that are very busy trying to make something work—but not without realizing that the economics of that new product or service can't accelerate their growth.

Which means that if you want to accelerate the growth of your business, then you have to make sure that the additional product or service you want to add possesses the right economics to justify adding it to your current offerings.

Trust me, this is not as obvious as it sounds. When I'm working with a company on their strategic plan, the owner/CEO and the members of their executive team will frequently throw out lots of growth ideas during the brainstorming part of the process. However, when we get to the evaluation part of the process and I begin asking them questions about the economics of those ideas (as well as the economics of their current products and services), the room always gets a whole lot quieter (and a lot of the suggested ideas get knocked off the board because they simply don't possess the right economics to drive significant growth).

c. **"Will this make our business more accessible to more people?"**

In other words, sometimes the additional product or service doesn't have to be a new and innovative product or service that no one has ever tried — sometimes it just needs to make your business more accessible to more people. For example, a church adding a second or third worship service on a Sunday morning, or a Saturday evening service, or a different kind of service at the same time, may be the additional "service" (pun intended) needed to get a growth curve started (However, adding a service without the infrastructure necessary to sustain that service—or, in the case of a church, without enough bodies in the room—can be disastrous).

I see this issue frequently in the practices of medical professionals like doctors, dentists, chiropractors, physical therapists, psychiatrists, etc. who tend to limit their office hours to times when THEY want to work (like M-R from 8:30 a.m. to 4:30 p.m.) which creates a built in constraint. In other words, if they would simply offer hours on Friday and/or Saturday or during the evening when most working people can show up, they could increase their service mix and potential revenue pool by up to 50%.

d. **"Will this help differentiate our business?"**

Since we've already discussed differentiation I won't belabor the point here, but I would encourage you to ask, "Why would we want to add products and/or services that, 'everyone' else is offering?'" That doesn't make sense. You want to be different.

Yes, you need to add products and services that your customers want, and yes you want to thwart the advances of your competitors, but from a strategic perspective, you want to make sure you're adding products and services to your mix that make you and your business the obvious vendor of choice in your market. You want your prospects to think, "Hey, we've got to use [ABC company] because they're the only ones who offer [XYZ]!"

e. **"Is this something that our target market passionately wants and is searching for?"**

Businesses all around the world offer new products and services everyday—and most of them don't sell very well. Why? In many cases, it's because they are products and services that the owners or CEOs likes, but which their prospects and customers don't have a passionate or irrational need/want for — or aren't actively searching for. So to avoid this trap, make sure you only offer new products and services which you know your target market passionately wants and is searching for.

For example, I recently had a conversation with my chiropractor who wanted to increase the total number of office visits to his chiropractic clinic per week. My first suggestion to him was to offer Saturday office hours. Why? Because, as someone who occasionally suffers from back pain, I know that if I injure my back on a Friday, I hate having to wait all weekend before I can see him. If he wasn't such a good friend, I know I would actively search out a chiropractor who had Saturday hours (and not just because of a potential pain issue, but because it's often hard to get away during normal office hours M-F).

In other words, I was suggesting a service add that his prospects and customers in his target market would passionately want and would be searching for. The good news is he took my suggestion and, surprise ... he quickly filled his Saturday hours. Why? Because people in pain are passionate about finding a solution and they don't want to have to wait days to find relief.

So, before you add a new product and/or service to your mix, make sure you go back and ask and answer these five questions. If you will, chances are you'll make a decision that can drive significant growth and help you break through your plateau.

2. You could add a new market

The second key strategic add for you to consider, besides adding new products and/or services to your current mix, would be to add new markets — either with your existing products and services or with any new products or services you might be adding to your current mix.

So, what kinds of new markets could you add?

a. **You could add a new geographical market.**

For example, it's not uncommon for a lot of small businesses to saturate their own local market in such a way that any growth gains they could get from their current target market would be marginal at best. In that case, expanding geographically to the next town or city or county or region is often a prerequisite for breaking through a growth plateau.

b. **You could add a new adjacent market.**

Let's say your business is in the document imaging world (taking documents, digitizing them, and storing them for easy retrieval) and your target market has been large regional hospitals. If you wanted to take your current products and services to an adjacent market, you could expand out to any of those businesses that work with large regional hospitals. For example, you could go after health insurance companies, pharmaceutical companies, biotech companies, large physicians' practices, etc. Those would all be considered adjacent markets to the large regional hospital market.

c. **You could expand into a new niche.**

Continuing our document imaging company example above, you could decide to go after a smaller niche in that medical market. Let's say, "Stand Alone Outpatient Surgery Centers", and try to own that niche so that you could become the dominant player in that market (vs. just one of many going after the larger regional hospital market). You could even take this idea down one more level to a micro-niche and go after all the small rural standalone outpatient surgery centers in your state.

d. **You could expand into a completely new and distant market.**

Of all the options, this is the most difficult to make work, but it is possible. For example, let's say you've acquired some expertise in the midst of engaging in your business (let's say you have a manufacturing business) and all of a sudden other CEOs and owners are asking you for advice about building their business like you have. If you started offering seminars and consulting services to other CEOs and businesses, you would, in essence, be offering new products and services to entirely new markets (i.e. clients in entirely new industries who wouldn't normally purchase what your manufacturing company produces).

3. You could add a new marketing channel

Another one of the more common mistakes that many small businesses make early on is declaring that they're a one channel marketing organization. The most frequently used phrase to describe this is, "We're a referral only business," (or, "We're a 100% referral-based business."). Now, I have nothing against referrals. In fact, I think they're one of the most powerful marketing strategies on the planet. My problem is that focusing on one channel alone is restrictive and therefore a constraint on growth.

Like far too many things in life, most people like to make choices into either/or choices vs. both/and choices. I'm clearly a both/and kind of guy. Either/or choices are rarely helpful. And, by definition, they're limiting choices. In other words, even if referrals are your best strategy, why would you ever want to limit your options to only one marketing channel?

Classic example. As I've mentioned, years ago I used to lead a large church. Like most churches, a lot of our new people came because a friend invited them (i.e. because of a referral). However, unlike most churches, we didn't limit our marketing to this one channel (i.e. we were not a referral-only business). In fact, I used a whole slew of marketing channels including advertising — especially the direct mail option of advertising.

What I find humorous these days is that even though it's been over six years since I left pastoral ministry I still meet people today who when they hear the name of my former church say, "Oh, you're the guy who used to send out all those mailers. I loved those! They were great!" Those mailers were key. They were a huge part of what drove the growth of my former church, a church which, during the decade of the 90's, grew an average of 30.5% PER YEAR for an entire decade.

Note: the current church I attend now gets its highest number of new guests through Google Adwords—another marketing option that most churches aren't taking advantage of. Just by adding this option (or a different option), more churches could be breaking through their plateaus.

Another one of the big either/or debates right now is between online and offline marketing—which is ridiculous. This is not an either/or choice, it's a both/and one. In other words, if you've traditionally been an offline marketer (direct mail, telemarketing, print advertising, etc.), then you could probably increase your reach and efforts by adding an online marketing channel.

On the other hand, if you've traditionally been an online marketer, you could probably increase your effectiveness and reach with some offline/more traditional marketing approaches. Remember, while email is cheaper, not everyone reads their email. Or maybe your email arrives when they're busy during the day and they never come back to read it. Or maybe your email got caught in a spam filter. If any of those happened, using a different channel, let's say a direct mail piece or a drive time radio spot or a tradeshow booth just might be the ticket you need to get them to hear and respond to your offer.

In light of this discussion on marketing channels, which marketing channels or strategies do you think you should consider adding to your current marketing mix?

If you're not sure of the different types of marketing channels, here's a quick list of the then major ones.

- *Referral strategies*
- *Networking strategies* (Events, Tradeshows, Associations/Groups, etc.)
- *Online strategies* (Pay-per-click, Banners, Website, Blog, SEO, etc.)
- *Writing strategies* (Books, Articles, Reports, Whitepapers, etc.)
- *Keep-in-touch strategies* (Ezines, Email, Phone Calls, Newsletters, etc.)

- *Speaking strategies* (Seminars, Keynotes, Talks, Training Sessions, Audio/mp3 Downloads, CDs, etc.)
- *Advertising* (Direct Mail, Radio, TV, Print Advertising, Tele-Marketing, Banners, Signage, etc.)
- *Publicity/PR strategies* (Press Releases, Community Involvement, Sponsorships, etc.
- *Joint Venture strategies* (Affiliate Programs, Value-Add Resellers, etc.)
- *Social Media* (Facebook, YouTube, Linkedin, etc.)

Regardless of what your marketing mix is right now, adding a new marketing strategy or channel to your mix, just may be the very thing you need to help you break through your current plateau!

And just in case I haven't made the case strong enough for you, as to why you might need to add an additional marketing channel to your business, consider the following statement from Michael Masterson and Mary Ellen Triby from their book, "Changing the Channel."

> *"A recent study by the Direct Marketing Association found that customers who bought from two channels rather than one were 20 to 60 percent more valuable to a company over time. And customers who bought from three channels versus one were 60 to 125 percent more valuable over time."*

In other words, adding an additional marketing channel or strategy to your marketing mix just may be the very thing that'll tip the scales in your favor so you can finally break through your plateau and get back on a double-digit growth curve.

Oh, and one last thought before we leave this chapter. When you work with your team to brainstorm what additional products and/or services you might want to add to your current product and/or service mix, as well as what new markets you may want to enter — may I encourage you to take the time to generate a lot of options. Too many leaders come up with a handful of ideas and then pick the best one out of the minimal number of ideas they came up with. However, if you want to build a fast growth business, you're going to want to push your team to generate lots of ideas because one of the keys to getting a great idea, is to have lots of ideas.

"The best way to get a good idea is to get lots of ideas." Linus
Pauling, Nobel Laureate in Physics

Even better, Doug Hall, who's company helps large companies be
more creative, made the following statement a few years ago that ought
to motivate you to want to generate as many ideas as possible for
growth. He simply said,

*"Companies with more choices for growth grow an average of 5.8
times faster than those with just a few ideas."*

Think about that! If you were to consistently generate lots of ideas
for growth, you could be growing 5.8 times faster than your
competitors! Even better, at 5.8 times faster growth, you'd have long left
your plateau behind in the dust.

So, if you want to get your business off your plateau and back on a
double-digit growth curve, make sure you add driver number seven to
your mix. Don't ride anything too long. Make sure you create a series of
S-curves by adding new products, services, markets and marketing
channels before you have to.

Application Driver #7: Addition

1. On a scale of 1-10 (high), how would you rate your business on its ability to innovate and add before it has to?

   _____

2. What was the last product or service you added to your product/service line? When? What were the results? Why?

3. What new product or service do you have coming online in the next 6-12 months?

4. Do you need to add any additional products and/or services to your current product/service mix?

5. Do you need to expand into new and/or additional markets at this point in time? If so, why?

6. What would be the next logical market to move into? Why?

7. What is your primary marketing channel? How long have you been riding it? What have the results been like over the past year?

8. What are your other primary marketing strategies (or tactics)?

9. Do you need to add a new marketing strategy or channel this year? If so, which one?

10. What do you think has been your major takeaway from this chapter?

11. In light of all the things you could add, what do you think is the first one you should add to accelerate your growth?

12. What can you do within the next day or two to get the ball rolling on that one thing?

Chapter 8
"Do It Once, Then Forget About It"

Driver #8: Systems

Because you're reading this book, chances are pretty high that you're an entrepreneur at heart. And the good news about being an entrepreneurial leader is that you're most likely an incredibly talented and driven individual. As such, I wouldn't be surprised that the people in your business are often amazed at your talents, insights, skills, determination, attitude, work ethic, etc. because you're a pretty remarkable person/worker.

And that is good news! Your talents and drive are probably the major reasons why your business (or organization) has achieved what it's achieved. Yet that good news is also bad news. Why? Because exceptional is not scalable.

You know this to be true because you've probably had trouble finding quality talent (meaning people like you) to hire. You've probably been frustrated that the people you've been able to hire just can't keep up with you or can't get things done like you or can't make things happen like you—and you're right—they can't.

What I say to entrepreneurial leaders like you all the time is, "If you could find more people like you, chances are you might be working for them." In other words, as an entrepreneurial leader, you have to give up on the idea that you can build a bigger, better, faster, and more profitable business on people like you. Even if you could find them, they wouldn't want to work for you. Just like you, they'd want to be in charge of their own company or organization.

So, what's the alternative? The alternative is to design your business on the ideal of, "Ordinary people doing ordinary work in such a way that they can create extraordinary and consistent outcomes for your customers and prospects." That is a scalable model. Exceptional is not. And the reason this is so important to our conversation in this book is because scalability is essential to building a fast growth business (or organization) that can break through any plateau.

In constraint theory, the problem solver (you) is always looking for the major constraints in a given system. By identifying and then removing (or reducing) the major constraint, the problem solver (you) can immediately release the natural flow in that system. When it comes to discovering the major constraints in most plateaued companies, one of them is invariably their reliance on exceptional talent — especially the talents of the founder/owner/CEO.

That said, this constraint problem isn't just related to you (the owner/founder/CEO), it's related to anyone in your organization who either possesses intellectual property that's unknown to others (i.e. they're the only person who knows how XYZ works or how XYZ work is done) or who possesses exceptional talent (i.e. where you become too dependent upon them as an individual).

As you can guess, whenever any business or organization becomes too dependent upon any one individual, that business or organization is vulnerable. What happens if that person leaves? Or dies? Or gets injured? Or sick? Or angry? Or loses their drive? You and your company are in trouble.

In addition, if you have an exceptional performer, not only has your organization probably become too dependent upon them — they probably haven't done what's necessary to groom additional talent to do what they do. So, again, you and your company are at risk

Now, this is not to suggest that you should not seek to hire the absolute best talent you possibly can — because you should! Talent is incredibly important. But regardless of what talent you acquire, you never want to build a business that is dependent upon exceptional talent in order to win in the marketplace — or that leaves intellectual property in the minds of a top performer (so that no one else has access to it).

The solution to this common problem is to move your business from an exceptional talent-based model to a systems-based model. Now, to be completely honest, using the phrase "systems-based" is a misnomer, because whether you intentionally create systems or you rely on capricious, ad-hoc and random performance, you're still using a system because even randomness is a system (i.e. even "I fly by the seat of my pants" is a system — just not a good system).

Now, one of the reasons why systems theory is so incredibly important to helping you get your business back on a growth curve is because systems theory always assumes that any observable problem in a system is a system's problem.

For example, it's not uncommon in a plateaued company to have some underperformers. Apart from having a systems perspective, the natural tendency for most leaders is to think, "Joe is the problem! If we just didn't have Joe on our team, we'd be closing more sales." But in systems thinking, Joe is not the problem, the system is the problem.

In other words, a leader who has a systems mindset, will tend to ask additional questions — questions like,

- Was the problem in our hiring process?
- Was it in our onboarding process?
- Are we not doing a good job in our on-going training?
- Is the problem Joe's manager?
- Is Joe getting the coaching he needs?
- Is Joe getting the right feedback?
- Has Joe been put on a performance plan?
- Does Joe know what exceptional performance looks like?
- Should Joe have been fired a long time ago?
- If so, why wasn't he?

This is the real power of a systems mindset — it causes us to ask better questions — which then leads us to think more clearly about what's underlying the presenting problem. Instead of taking the easy option ("Fire Joe"), a systems perspective helps you and me uncover the underlying systemic problems that need to be resolved in order to prevent this problem from occurring again in the future.

Likewise, let's say you have a sales conversion problem. Using a systems mindset you wouldn't immediately assume the problem is Sally. Instead you'd look at all of systems connected to Sally and sales conversion. For example, you might ask,

- Is our lead generation system producing enough leads?
- Is it producing highly qualified leads?
- Are we sending out the right marketing messages to the right targets?
- Have we provided the right training for our sales reps?
- Have we tested our sales scripts?
- Is there something in the sales cycle that's broken?
- Do our sales reps have access to the information they need in order to close a high percentage of sales?

Again, this is why systems thinking and systems design are so incredibly important and valuable to you — especially when you're stuck on a plateau. There is a reason why you're stuck. So own that. Then begin to unleash systems thinking and design to help you, first of all, fix the systems that are broken and then secondly, optimize the systems that are currently working.

Once you own systems thinking as a part of your culture, it really will change everything for your business. Why? Because from this point forward, everyone should be working on creating systems — all the time — about everything. And once they're created, your people should be testing and optimizing each of those systems so that they keep getting better and better.

Now, before we take a look at how to create systems for your business, here are a few more thoughts about systems you'll want to master.

1. *A system is a group of independent items (actions/people/ things) that interact together to achieve a goal.*

    In other words, a system is designed to accomplish something. For example, the ecosystem of our planet was designed in such a way that human life can be sustained on it. Likewise, when you set out to design a system, you should always begin with a clear understanding of what the goal/result is that you want to achieve. And the more clear and specific your goal/result is, the better your chances are that you'll design a system that will achieve what you want.

For example, if your goal is a generic, "We want to generate more leads," that's okay but technically, if you generate one more lead than you're currently receiving, that would fulfill your goal. However, if your goal was, "We want to generate 250 new high quality leads each month that will convert at a 70% conversion rate," you'll probably create an entirely different (and more profitable) system.

In other words, systems aren't just about writing down the steps taken in a procedure so that someone else can do them. Systems are about achieving a goal or result that you want to attain. Far too few leaders get that distinction.

2. *Systems aren't designed to constrain behavior – they're designed to ensure consistent and predictable results.*

In other words, you don't want a customer's experience with your company to be dependent on whether or not Betty or Sally picks up the phone. You want to know that—regardless of who's answering the phone—whenever anyone calls your company they're going to have a great experience.

Note: this doesn't mean you can't create a system without individualization or variation built into it. Nor, does it mean you're only allowed to hire robots.

Rather it simply means that you want to create a business where you can guarantee that the people who interact with your business (or organization) can have a consistent and predictable experience—regardless of who's delivering the service. Or, if your system is internal, that the people who are engaged in completing a task can deliver a consistent and predictable result—regardless of who's doing that task.

3. *Apart from measuring the results of a system, you can never be sure if you're obtaining optimal results.*

While you may think you're obtaining optimal results, you can never be sure unless you're consistently measuring. Or to put it another way, in order to know you're obtaining an optimal result, you have to have previous results that you're measuring your new result against. This means that whenever you're designing a new system—and it's a system you want to optimize (like a lead generation system) — you want to create some kind of measurement process as part of the system.

For example, let's say you're creating a new system to follow up inactive customers. In your mind, you think a letter and a follow up call would be the best one-two strategy. But is it? How do you know?

- Is a two-step "campaign" really the best?
- Would a three or five or seven step campaign be better?
- Would email be better than a letter and a follow up call?
- How about an email, a postcard, a letter, another email, and then a phone call, followed up by a hand-written thank you card?

Bottom line, you just don't know what's the optimal system until you test and measure the results.

At the end of the day, the better your business is at creating and optimizing systems, the better your business will be and the faster it'll grow! If you want to break through your current plateau, you not only need to create a culture of systems thinking and design, you also need to fix or eliminate the systems that are holding you back.

So, how do you go about creating new and better systems? Here's a simple five-step process that you can begin using today that'll help you build more and better systems.

1. **Clarify the issue you want to work on.**

    Out of all the possible systems you could create, which one do you want to work on right now? Note: This is easier said than done.

    For example, you could work on something that's broken. You could work on something that drives you nuts and makes you hate your job. You could work on something that consumes too much of your time and ought to be delegated. You could work on systemizing your most important work. Or most profitable work. Or least profitable work. Or most stressful work. Or most routine work. Etc.

    But whatever you choose to work on, choose to work on one issue at a time. Don't try to fix your whole business all at once.

Remember the Pareto principle (the 80/20 rule). You want to choose an issue that is currently a major constraint in your business. While there are literally hundreds of systems you could create, why waste your time creating systems that won't move the needle for your business.

Then, once you identify the issue you want to work on, you'll want to create great clarity about the goal/result/outcome that you want to achieve. For example, if the problem in your business is that your people aren't converting enough leads into customers, then make sure you come up with a very clear goals statement like, "We want our sales conversion process to convert at least 60% of all prospect inquires into actual sales."

2. **Design a Prototype Solution**

Once you have clarity about the result you want to obtain, the next step is for you personally (alone or with your team) to design the first prototype solution. Don't worry about perfection, just get something down on paper. You can tweak it later. If you'd like to download a paper template for creating a system, which I refer to as an Activity Action Plan, just go to the Free Helps section of my website--under the Free tab at www.WiredToGrow.com and download the template.

If you'd prefer to create your own system's template, here are the key ingredients to a good systems template.

- The name of the activity (for example, with your website, you might write "How to Update a Web Page on Our Website").
- The goal or result desired (for example, with your coffee service you might write, "To have fresh hot coffee available for all staff and guests between the hours of 8:00 a.m. and 5:00 p.m. Monday – Friday.")
- Who's responsible for this activity (Note: Use the position, "VP of Marketing," not the person, "Jill").
- Who do they report to (Again, use the position versus the person).
- What resources are required for successful completion of this activity
- The frequency of how often this system should be utilized (daily, weekly, monthly, whenever, etc.)

- The actual process of steps (which should include what the step is, who should complete that step, and by when)
- Any psychological or physiological items (for example, any mindset or attitudinal issues)
- What the standards and expectations are for successful completion of that activity (for ex. "You will leave the conference room completely cleaned--with the chairs neatly arranged around the table, the table top completely cleaned off — wiped off if necessary, and all garbage in the garbage can").
- Finally, you may want to attach anything that could help another person complete that activity. For example, a flow chart or pictures or a video or a diagram or a FAQ or a worksheet or a template or a mp3 or a checklist.

Then, once you have version one of your prototype solution, go back through and try to follow your own directions — personally. Chances are you'll catch a lot of things you didn't catch the first time. Why? Because most of us do what we do instinctively — which means that there are a number of things we assume everyone should know — but they don't. So, following your own directions will often help you catch a number of missing pieces to your system.

3. **Implement the System**

The next step is critical. You want to actually train someone to do the activity. Most owners and CEOs prefer to dump than delegate. But if you want to turn your business around, you've got to become more of a coach who delegates vs. a CEO who dumps.

As you train someone else to use the prototype you've created, you'll want to watch them follow your system instructions. Why? Because, invariably, you're going to find a number of items you'll need to modify or add to your prototype system. What seems so obvious to you, probably won't to others.

4. **Measure the Results**

As the military maxim goes, "No plan survives the first encounter with an enemy." No matter how "perfect" a system may look on paper, reality usually dictates that something won't work as planned. Therefore, it's essential that you measure the results you're getting so you can effectively evaluate the system as it's designed.

Once you know what's not working (based on your measurements), you can simply make adjustments to the system until the system itself produces a consistent and predictable outcome — regardless of who's using the system.

5. **Optimize the System**

The fifth and final stage of systems building has no real end point — other than when you decide enough is enough. Why? Because perfection doesn't exist. Virtually everything can be improved upon.

Also, as you're seeking to optimize your systems, don't forget to look for little tweaks. For example, in retail, there's a huge difference in response if a sales person walks up to a customer and asks, "May I help you?" vs. "Have you been here before?" Those two questions don't seem to be all that different, but the response levels are dramatic.

When someone asks, "May I help you?" most people say, "No." and the conversation ends right then and there. However, when someone asks, "Have you ever been here before?" regardless of the answer, the conversation can continue. For the person who says, "No," the sales person can say, "Well welcome to our store. Even better, we have a special going on right now for our first time guests ..." And to the person who says, "Yes," the sales person can say, "Great. I don't know if you're aware of this, but we're currently offering a special sale to our regular customers ..."

Of course, the only way to know for sure that there's a difference in response between those two questions is to test and measure — which, if you become a systems person will become two of your favorite words — that is, if you want to grow a bigger, better, faster and more profitable business!

Well, that should be more than enough to get you started on creating better systems for your business. But remember, if you want to break through your plateau, you've got to create a culture where systems thinking and design is a part of the culture. Systems design isn't a once in a while thing, it needs to become a way of life for your business.

And what you'll find is that the more systems you create, and the better those systems are, and the more those systems are being optimized — the faster your business will grow, the more consistent the experience will be for your customers, and the more you'll enjoy being the owner/CEO/founder of your business since you'll no longer have to do as much work as you used to do. So what are you waiting for? Go create a system today!

Applications for Driver #8: Systems

1. On a scale of 1-10 (high), how would you rate your company on its ability to create and improve systems? _____

2. What percentage of your "systems" (meaning everything you do for your business) do you think are actually documented? _____

3. What do you think hinders you from creating more systems?

4. How can you overcome those issues?

5. If you could pick one thing YOU need to systemize to get it off your plate, what would that one item be?

6. If you were to pick the top three systems that YOUR COMPANY needs to fix first, what would they be?

7. If you were to pick one from that list, which one would it be? Why?

8. Start working that issue/system through the five-step process laid out in this chapter.

9. What do you think was your major takeaway from this chapter? Why?

10. What is the first thing you need to do within the next 24 hours to get a system design project started?

11. Don't forget to download the Activity Action Guide Template from my website at www.WiredToGrow.com (under Free > Free Tools and Helps)

Chapter 9
"Add CMO (Chief Morale Officer) to Your Title"

Driver #9: Morale

Have you ever been a part of a winning or high performance team? If so, what was the atmosphere like on your team? Chances are the morale of your team was incredibly high. It probably felt like you couldn't lose.

On the other hand, have you ever been part of a losing or low performance team? If so, what was the atmosphere like? Chances are exactly the opposite of the high performance team.

Now, if that's true (and it is), then why do you think most leaders who want to build bigger, better, faster and more profitable businesses don't pay more attention to this incredibly important and critical driver of high performance teams?

I'm constantly amazed at how many leaders don't pay more attention to this driver every week (let alone every day). It's like a blind spot. It's there, but they can't see it. And that's unfortunate. Why? Because morale is everything whenever you're leading an organization! I love the way John Maxwell puts it,

"When Big Mo' is with you, you can do no wrong. But when Big Mo' is against you, you can do no right!"

Morale/momentum is a very big deal. And apart from paying attention to it every day/week, I can unequivocally state that you are hindering the growth of your business (or organization).

One of the unfortunate realities of leading any group of people is knowing that somewhere between 40 – 50% of employee effort is discretionary. You know this to be true. You can hand an assignment to Joe — who will methodically get the steps done, slowly, with a bad attitude, while watching the clock and doing the bare minimum that qualifies for getting the task done. Or you can hand the very same assignment to Angela — who will take what you've given her, make it her own, get it done quickly, and add some special little "something" to it.

Same assignment. Same boss. Same directions. Same due date. Radically different results. Why? Because Angela's morale/attitude/ excitement (or whatever else you want to call it) was much higher than Joe's. Trust me, 40-50% of all employee effort is discretionary. One of the unfortunate realities of life on this planet is that very few employees are self-motivated — which means that the vast majority of the people you employ will need someone outside of them (i.e. you their leader/manager) to help them produce at their maximum output.

At its core, this is a leadership issue. Why? Because this is what leaders do. Unfortunately, most "pure managers" don't get this because they're usually too focused on the task and making sure the task gets done. "Joe, here's the assignment. Here's what you need. Make sure it's done by Tuesday at noon."

But what great leaders know is that people come bundled together with emotions and feelings. They're not automatons carrying out rote tasks. They're human beings who do what they do for a reason. They do what they like to do, the way they like to do it, with the people they like doing it with — and for the person whom they like doing it for.

So in the case of Joe, if he's not "feeling the love," from his boss, or if he's not excited about his company, or if he's worried about an upcoming review, or if he's in conflict with another co-worker, or if he's having trouble at home, or if he's enduring some kind of physical pain, or if he's upset about a decision the company made, etc. then chances are very low that Joe is going to complete the task well — and great leaders know this.

This is why great leaders always pay attention to morale and the emotions of their people. Why? Because they know that the failure to do so can be devastating to the productivity and performance of their team. In fact, I love the way Tim Sanders puts this,

> *"If the average employee has a pit in his stomach instead of a song in his heart, your profits will go down."*

I cannot state this any stronger ... Morale is a very big deal! If you want to get your business off its current plateau, then you've got to pay massive attention to this driver. And the good news is that if you do, it can make a significant difference in your business (or organization) in a rather short span of time.

Remember, leadership is all about leverage — which means that if you want to get the maximum amount of leverage out of your people, in the shortest amount of time, then you're going to want to pay consistent daily and weekly attention to morale.

What I tell my clients all the time (while licking and then lifting my index finger like I'm checking the wind or temperature) is, "You should be testing the temperature of your business or organization every day — or at a minimum--every week. And if at any time that you do that you sense that morale is not at its peak, do something to ratchet it back up."

Why? Because when morale is lost, it takes a lot to get it back on track. So, you always want to pay a lot of attention to morale because it's infinitely easier to bring up a little dip in morale than it is to resurrect dead morale. Plus, if morale influences employee performance (and it does), and if it is the job of the leader to produce results through people (and it is) then, as a leader, you can't afford to let morale slip at all.

This is true all the time — but it is immeasurably more important whenever a business (or organization) is plateaued — because plateaus are morale killers. In other words, if your business has been plateaued for any length of time you've got a major morale problem. And the longer you've been on a plateau, the more attention you have to pay to morale — over a very long time.

So, what can you do to get morale back up? Well, here are a few ideas to get you started.

1. **Make sure YOUR morale is high**. It's what I call, "Leader Draft."

   This is the single biggest factor to influencing high morale because morale isn't really taught — it's caught. In fact, let me share with you how the truth of this principle was driven home to me several years ago.

   As I mentioned before, I used to be the pastor of a church in Germantown MD that grew from two families to two thousand people. During the decade of the 90's, we grew an average of 30.5% per year for those ten years — which means that growth was just a way of life for us.

   But midway through that decade, during one spring we didn't grow — we flatlined. This had never happened to us. So I started asking questions of myself and of others, "What's going in? Is there something going on that I'm unaware of? Are we doing something wrong?" Etc.

   But no one, including me, had any answers. So, one day during a staff meeting I asked my staff once again, "Does anyone have any ideas for why we're not growing this Spring?" Finally, one of my staff members took a risk and said, "Bruce, I think it might be you." I responded, "Why do you think that?" And he responded with a statement I've never forgotten.

   He said, "Bruce, I think you underestimate how much we all draft our energy off of you. Over the last month, you've been tired and burned out, and I think that's affected all of us." And he was right. That was the day I realized that as a leader, if I wanted to build a fast growing organization, I could never be "down" when I was with my people.

   By the way, it wasn't that I was telling people, "I'm tired and burned out." It's that they could sense it, just like people sense expectations. They noticed that my level of energy had dropped, and therefore it dropped throughout the whole organization.

So, my encouragement to you is, if morale is low, check yourself first. What's your morale level like? What's your energy level like? How excited are you about the work you and your business/organization are engaged in? How full is your emotional tank? If you want to raise the morale level of your organization, I know of no better or faster way to do that than this, to raise your own morale!

Note: If you want some ideas on how to lift your own excitement and enthusiasm about your business, you'll want to watch this video on my site at

http://wiredtogrow.com/whats-your-hustle-factor/

2.   **Become a master caster.**

Apart from modeling positive morale and excitement for the work you do, the second most powerful morale builder on the planet is vision casting.

Unfortunately, most business owners and CEOs don't get this — or if they do get it, they don't practice it regularly enough. Casting vision isn't a once a year, at the annual meeting, kind of practice. Nor is it a once every six-months, "I should write something with that 'vision thing' in it for our newsletter," kind of practice.

Real vision-casting is an every day, every week, every month kind of practice. It's something that should be front and center every time you encounter an employee or lead a meeting or write a letter or give a speech. In fact, my rule is that you can never cast vision too much.

Why? Because people leak vision ... every day. You know this to be true because the same thing happens to you. You go to a conference. You get inspired. You come back to work. And the next day you're wondering, "Now, what was I so excited about yesterday?" It happens to all of us.

So everyday, if you want to be a great leader who inspires people to do great work and to accomplish great things, you need to be thinking, "How can I cast vision to inspire this person (or this group of people)?"

For example, let's say you're practicing your MBWA and you encounter Barbara, who works in purchasing (and your company is in the biotech market). After talking with Barbara for a few moments you say, "Barbara, I just want to take a moment to say how thankful I am for what you're doing. I'm sure there are days when you feel like all you're doing is processing paperwork. But I just want to remind you that that is not what you're doing. What you're doing is helping to change the lives of people who suffer from [XYZ disease]. Every time you process an order to make sure that our scientists have what they need when they need it so they can stay focused on creating new drug therapies, you are helping to change the lives of people. You, Barbara, are making a difference. And I hope you never forget that."

Now, that didn't take very long, did it? But what do you think is going to happen to Barbara's work that day? It's going to skyrocket! Her metrics are going to blow through the roof! Her owner/CEO just took a few minutes with her, and cast vision for her, that she'll treasure—at least for the next few days. And then she'll need to be reminded of that again and again. Why? Because vision leaks! And it leaks every day.

When you're with groups, the best way to cast vision is with stories. So, always be on the look out for good stories. In fact, I used to ask my staff for stories every week so I could then pass them along to others (by the way, that's a great way to make others think you know everything that's going on. Why? Because when you're sharing stories from all over your company, most people think you must know everything that's going on).

For example, let's say you heard about Mohammed who went above and beyond the call to fix a customer problem. At your next meeting (or in a blog or email) you ought to tell that story to everyone--and then link it to a core value or a strategic initiative to get the vision-casting part in.

For example, let's say you're having a company meeting and during that meeting you say, "Hey, yesterday in our executive staff meeting, Jacquie, shared with me that a member of her team, Mohammed, went above and beyond the call to fix a customer problem this week. The basic storyline is that Mrs. Smith called in to our call center at 4:59 p.m. on Monday complaining about how one of our installers installed her new refrigerator — but forgot to connect the water line for the automatic icemaker. Now, as you know, the normal procedure in that case would be to call the installation center and have someone go out tomorrow and fix it first thing in the morning since it was now past 5:00 p.m. However, Mohammed decided to do something he didn't have to do, he offered to stop by Mrs. Smith's house on his way home and make the connection himself.

In my book, that means that Mohammed is one of our band of heroes. He didn't have to do what he did. But when he did, he lifted up core value #2 (on customer service). When we started this company seven years ago, we started with the idea that customers would use us over the big box stores because they'd value our customer service difference — and Mohammed just made that vision come true in the life of Mrs. Smith on Oak Street. So, Mohammed, job well done! I'm glad to have you on the team!"

Making a statement like that only takes about a minute or two out of your meeting, but what an impact it will have! Not only will Mohammed's morale go up — almost everyone else's morale in that room will go up as well.

Plus, by sharing that story, you would have just cast vision for everyone in that room as to what great customer service looks like. Any way you add it up, vision-casting is incredibly powerful.

So make sure you use it at least every week, if not every day. In fact, I'd recommend you make it part of your job description. Job #1 = Cast vision.

3. **Eliminate all unWOW.**

Every workplace/work environment has certain things that employees don't like that hinder morale. Whatever those things are — eliminate them. For example, I frequently walk into office spaces that depress me. It could be carpets that haven't been cleaned in years or walls that haven't been painted since the Vietnam war or cloth cubicles with big stains on the fabric that stem from a Christmas party five years ago or flickering lights or ten year old computers or missing or water damaged ceiling panels etc. All of those items affect morale. And the amazing thing is that, from a cost basis, most of them aren't that expensive to correct. But more importantly, from a productivity standpoint, they're actually very inexpensive to fix and very costly to not fix.

However, unWOW isn't just related to just physical things in the work environment. UnWOW could be related to a policy or procedure or to a compensation issue or to a hypercritical manager, etc. For example, I've watched classic 8:00 a.m. - 5:00 p.m. managers "kill" their creatives by requiring them to all be at the office by 8:00 a.m. Some creatives will work in that environment, but a lot of them will wake up at 2:00 a.m. with an idea and then spend the next four hours, while the manager is sleeping, working on that idea. In a business that uses creatives, requiring them to all be at work by 8:00 a.m. everyday could easily be an unWOW. Switching to a flex time schedule and holding all staff meetings at 10:00 a.m. vs. 8:00 a.m. would be simple changes that could have a radical impact on staff morale.

In other words, as the Chief Morale Officer of your company, you should continually be looking for ways to eliminate anything that is an unWOW in your work environment in order that you can automatically unleash a higher level of productivity and love for your company among your employees.

4.   **Practice MBWA**

Since Tom Peters, in 1982, made Managing By Walking Around (MBWA) part of the lexicon of managers/leaders, it hasn't been a novel idea. However, for most business leaders — especially those leading plateaued companies — it's merely a familiar phrase, not a frequent practice. However, by moving MBWA from knowledge to practice, you can radically change your company's morale.

In fact, one owner/CEO of a company in the document management world heard me talk about MBWA at a two-day conference I led on accelerated growth issues. A little over a month later I was on a follow up conference call with the attendees of that conference when this specific owner/CEO said, "One of the first things I did when I returned from the two day conference was I started practicing MBWA with my employees every morning at the start of the work day. And I can't tell you what a difference it's made in the morale here at my company. It's been remarkable."

Now, to help you understand why this made such a huge difference in his company, you ought to know that in the document management world, the executives and the production people tend to be very separate. The owners and top executives (a small group of people) tend to be focused on sales and marketing, they tend to be college educated, and they tend to be very "white collar." On the other hand, the production people (usually a much larger group of people), tend to be very task oriented, they tend to be less educated, and they tend to be very "blue collar." In other words, there's often a huge gap between the two groups. So, by this owner/CEO taking the time every morning to "walk the shop," and taking the time to talk with the hourly "laborers," every day, and getting to know them and their lives — morale skyrocketed — as did his company's productivity and profits — all from one simple idea — that it's a good thing for a leader to "walk among his/her people."

So don't underestimate the power of this practice. Regular use of MBWA really can change a company and get it back on a growth curve.

5. **Spread Leader Dust.**

Remember the story of Peter Pan? Remember Tinkerbell and her pixie dust? Do you remember what pixie dust could make people do? Exactly! It could make them fly! Well, that's what leader dust is all about.

As you're practicing MBWA, you want to make sure you're not just talking about last night's TV shows or sports scores, you want to make sure you're encouraging your people with very specific words of encouragement.

For example, in my former career, while most pastors would be in their church service during the first half of the service, I would usually be walking the halls, spreading leader dust, encouraging our volunteers for all of their hard work. Every week it would require between 125 -150 volunteers just to pull off a Sunday service. So, to me, walking the halls and encouraging the hearts of volunteers was the absolute best use of my time. It didn't take a lot of time. But the pay off was huge.

One of the things most of us as leaders underestimate is how much what we say matters to other people. If you're at all like me, you know all your own junk and probably don't take yourself all that seriously. You're just another human being. But to your people, you're the leader/owner/CEO/Executive Director/Senior Pastor/Managing Partner and what you say matters. So, taking the time to say something encouraging means a lot.

Of course, the best way to spread leader dust is to write it or put it on something they can keep. I used to have my assistant put thank you cards on my desk to remind me to send out cards to encourage people. Six months or a year later, I could walk into someone house and there you'd find that "Thank You" card on their refrigerator. One card. Two minutes. Three sentences. And someone's still living off it, six months later.

In fact, one of my favorite stories about this was in the early years of our church, when we didn't have any money, I used to give out what we called, "The Copper Top Awards." Now, the Copper Tops weren't very fancy and they didn't cost a whole lot. In fact, they were simply a Styrofoam cup, turned upside down, with a penny on top of it, and an award name written on the side of the cup with a permanent pen marker. Yet, I could visit the home of a Copper Top award winner several YEARS later, and they'd still have that Copper Top award on a shelf somewhere in their home—which clearly demonstrates to me how much most people are dying for some affirmation and encouragement.

So never underestimate the power of Leader Dust. Spread it liberally every day and you'll make your people fly. William James was absolutely correct when he wrote,

"The deepest human need is the need to be appreciated."

6. **Start a Company Blog**

    I think this is one of the most underutilized vision-casting opportunities by owners and CEOs today. Why? Because a company blog has the potential to be a phenomenal Leader

Dust tool. Whenever praise and encouragement are written down they become more powerful. But when it's both written down AND made public, it becomes even more powerful.

So, while it's nice that Janice received a handwritten "Thank You" (or "I Appreciate You") card from you, it's even more powerful that you posted a story about her and how her negotiation skills with a new vendor just saved your company $29,452. Or how Donald and Patrick took it upon themselves to organize a community outreach drive that resulted in a donation of $6,174 to a local non-profit. Or how Sally and her team went above and beyond the call of duty to exceed the requirements of an RFP and they won the contract.

Where can you post those stories so everyone can see and hear them? You got it. Your company blog. If you make your blog a Leader Dust opportunity, everyone in your company will be reading it. And morale will skyrocket.

Note: If you think that writing a blog is beyond you, it's not. If you can use Microsoft Word, you can write a blog post. Don't let the technology get in the way of you bragging on your people. Start a company blog today!

7. **Care about your people's lives outside of work**

I'm guessing that you're somewhat familiar with the phrase, "People don't care how much you know until they know how much you care." Well, that's clearly true in the workplace. Your workers/employees/team members (or whatever you call them) want to know that they matter to you — that they're more than just a number or part of an economic engine.

So, if you want to make morale soar, you'll want to demonstrate that you actually care about what happens to them outside of work. Know their spouse/partner's name and what they do. Know their kids' names and what kinds of activities they're engaged in. Know what hobbies they participate in. Know where they like to vacation. Know their family ancestry. Know if they're religious or not, etc. All of those points of interest and connection matter — and if you know them and show you care about them, they'll be far more motivated to produce the best they can because they know that they have a leader who cares about them — and not just what they can deliver for the company.

8. Know what motivates the different people on your team

This is another one of those, "Duh! Isn't this obvious?" points. But it's not. Everyone is motivated by different things. Some people are motivated by public praise, others by private. Some are motivated by presents, while others are motivated by time spent together. Some are motivated by new responsibilities, while others only by money. Some are motivated by titles and positions, others could care less. Some are motivated by challenge, others are motivated by routine. Everyone is motivated differently.

So, as the Chief Morale Officer, one of your jobs it to observe your people in action, as well as to understand their personalities and their likes and dislikes in order that you can discern who on your team is motivated by what so you can motivate them based on what motivates them, not you.

If you want some real help with this, you'll want to check out my program entitled *Personality Type Leadership: How to Lead People Who Don't Think, Act and Feel Like You* (www.PersonalityTypeLeadership.com)

Another idea is to always pay attention to their conversations. For example, if you notice that Mark always talks about Top Chef the night after an episode airs, you can probably guess he's a foodie. If on the other hand, you notice that Joan is always talking about the DIY network, you can probably guess that she loves doing home projects. Knowing the difference between those two means that you'll probably be better able to reward them with something they'd like (dinner for two at the hot new restaurant in town for Mark and a gift certificate to Home Depot or Lowes for Joan).

Any way you add it up, morale matters--and even more so in any business (or organization) that has been plateaued for any length of time. If you want to get your company back on a double-digit growth curve, then you've got to integrate high morale into your culture.

Applications for Driver #9: Morale

1. On a scale of 1-10 (high), how would you evaluate the current morale of your company? _____

2. What evidence do you have for the answer you just wrote in above?

3. Do you own the responsibility for morale in your company? Do you see yourself as the Chief Morale Officer?   Yes or No (circle one) Why or why not?

4. What's your morale like right now? What's your excitement level?

5. On a scale of 1-10 (high), what score would your people give you on your level of morale? Why?

6. What can you do to pick up your morale and enthusiasm?

7. What are some of the unWOWs for your employees?

8. Which ones could you change quickly that would have a significant impact on them?

9. What is something you can cast vision for this week?

10. Who do you need to thank this week?

11. Make a list of your direct reports. What motivates each of them? How are they different from you?

12. What is your major takeaway from this chapter?

13. What is one thing you can do this week to improve the level of morale in your business?

Chapter 10
"Never Forget, Even in Business, It's All About Love!"

Driver #10: Love

Of the ten drivers, this may seem to be the outlier, the one where you're scratching your head thinking, "What is he thinking? Love? What's love got to do with it?" Answer: everything. But rather than tell you why, let me share with you a few comments made by a couple of fellow entrepreneurial leaders about this driver called love.

For example, let's take Steve Jobs. Now, I don't know if you've ever read Steve Jobs' commencement address that he gave back in 2005 at Stanford University, but in the middle of that speech he made an interesting comment about love as a driver in business. He said,

> "I'm convinced that the only thing that kept me going was that I loved what I did. You've got to find what you love. And that is as true for your work as it is for your lovers. Your work is going to fill a large part of your life, and the only way to be truly satisfied is to do what you believe is great work. And the only way to do great work is to love what you do."

By the way, that's not the only time he made this point. On another occasion, when he was discussing the subject of success at work, he made the following statement.

"If you really look at the ones that end up being successful in the eyes of society and those that don't, oftentimes it's because the ones that are successful loved what they did so they persevered when it got really tough, and the ones that didn't love it quit, because they're sane, right? Who would want to put up with this stuff if you don't love it."

In other words, the idea of love as a driver in business wasn't just a nice fluffy thing for Steve to throw into a commencement address, it's really what he thought. Or to put it another way, love wasn't a soft concept for Steve, it was hard. It had real practical value for what drove him and Apple to become the most valuable company on the planet.

His counterpart, Bill Gates, who's typically a little less verbose than Steve, when talking about work simply said,

"I could do this forever." Bill Gates

It's all about love — and not just in the tech world. You can go outside the tech arena and see virtually the same thing in any industry. For example, in Hollywood, listen to what Tom Cruise has to say about love as a driver.

"I love what I do. I take great pride in what I do. And I can't do something halfway, three-quarters, nine-tenths. If I'm going to do something, I go all the way."

Katherine Graham, the former publisher of the Washington Post, once put it this way,

"To love what you do and feel that it matters…how could anything be more fun?"

Or Brian Tracy, one of the top motivational and business growth speakers on the planet, put it this way.

"Throughout all my decades of helping people reach their goals, I found one common trait among the top 1%. They all LOVE what they do."

Any way you add it up, one of the great drivers of all highly successful fast growth leaders is that they love what they do, they love their employees, and they love their products and services. And it is that culture of love that makes all the activities in their businesses work that much better.

From my perspective, love is one of those rarely discussed business "secrets" that really should get more press because it does make a significant difference in the growth of any organization. It doesn't guarantee growth because it is possible to love what you do and not have a growing organization, but it's rare to find a fast growth business or organization where the leaders aren't passionate about what they do.

To help you see how important this subject is, let's take a look at each of the three main love categories and see how they might be able to help you get your business (or organization) back on a growth curve.

1. **A passion/love for your products and/or services**

    It's not unusual for an owner/entrepreneur to start out with a passionate love for their products and/or services — only to see that passion lapse over time. And as you've hopefully picked up in this book, whatever is true for you becomes true for your business. If you've lost your love for your products and/or services, that will, by definition, affect everyone else connected with your business.

    On the other hand, when you're passionately in love with your products and/or services, it changes everything and everyone. I remember a few years ago when I injured my back, I had to remain lying flat on my back for about three days. After the first day or so I was bored and flipping through the channels on my TV when I came across Emeril Lagasse (this was back when he was on the Food Network). As I watched him — even though, at the time, I didn't cook, I was drawn to his show.

    Why? Because his energy and passion for what he did was effusive — and contagious. Shortly after watching him, I decided to try my hand at cooking and guess what? I found that I loved cooking (i.e. because of Emeril's passion, I took up cooking at age 45). But, and here's the point, I never would have even tried cooking if it wasn't for Emeril Lagasse's passion for the work he does. For him, it's all about love. In fact, when he's talking about food he'll often say, "It's a love thing!"

    Unfortunately, when I encounter leaders of businesses or organizations that have been stuck on a plateau, I usually find the opposite of that kind of zeal and passion. They're usually exhausted and tired people, frustrated that things aren't working out the way they had hoped, and what was once a passion for them, has become nothing more than a job. The twinkle has left the house. The thrill is gone. The lights are out. And love is nowhere to be found.

Yet, found it must be because love is critical to getting any business back on a growth curve — if for no other reason than what Steve Jobs alluded to in his comments — that love is what causes someone to persevere and tolerate all the junk that you have to wade through if you want to build a great business.

2. **A passion/love for your employees**

I'm always surprised when I encounter leaders who don't "love" (i.e. in a non-physical, non-sexual way) their employees. These are the people whom they've hired and whom they're leveraging to get more work done. Without them — the business doesn't exist any longer — or the leader is truly buried under responsibility.

If there was ever a group of people to love (outside of your family), it should be your employees. And whenever you love someone, one of the first fruits of that love should always be that you want the best for them. In fact, I love the way Boyd Clarke puts this. He said,

> *"I have always believed that the purpose of the corporation is to be a blessing to the employees."*

I love that line! In other words, the purpose of a business is not just to allow us to use our employees to get what we want (for ex. more money), it's also about us being a blessing to them (paying them well, providing for them and their families, helping them get their kids through school, offering them a chance to do what they were created to do — while using their gifts and talents to benefit others, offering them a chance to feel good about themselves and letting them know they're making a difference in someone else's life).

Along this same line of thinking, another one of my favorite quotes on this subject comes from Keith Dunn, President of McGuffey's Restaurants who said,

"If you don't care about your restaurant, then don't worry about how you treat your employees. But if you want to halt turnover, cut food cost, build sales and increase profits, you have to love your people to death."

Again, I love that! Why? Because he's right. One of the things that most people miss about love is that it's difficult to fake. Most employees can sense when our love for them is authentic or when it's just another tactic to improve performance.

Oh, and one last thing to remember about love — it's a verb. Love is something we do. It's not primarily an emotion, it's primarily an action. It's not primarily something we say, it's primarily something we demonstrate.

So, if your company is low on the love quotient, you may want to start by doing a few things for your employees — little things — that let them know that you care about them and that they matter to you. For example, observing that your administrative assistant likes to occasionally treat herself to a Starbucks Extra-hot, Venti Caramel Macchiato with Soy Milk is one of those little things that lets her know you care ... when you surprise her with one.

3.   **A passion/love for your customers**

The third leg of this love triangle is your customer. Do you love them? Are you excited about solving their problems? Do you get excited when you get to meet them? Or has that waned for you?

In most plateaued companies, it's waned. Customers are either a bother ("Business sure would be more fun if we didn't have to deal with customers!") or a means to an end (i.e. people we need to extract as much value out of as possible in order to make our numbers this week/month/quarter/year). And whenever that happens — when customers become either a bore or a means to an end--just like with employees, it ends up being transmitted to them. They can feel/sense it from us--and our employees.

I love the way Dave Dauten puts it when he writes,

"Here's my formula for business success, and it rates as an IBP, an Important Business Principle: If you don't love your customer, get another customer. If you can't find a customer to love, get another business."

That's great advice. Getting up off a plateau is a lot of hard work. And if you don't love the people you're offering a solution to then maybe creating an exit strategy is a good place to start. So, either fall in love with your prospects and customers again — or find another business.

Oh, and one last thought about customer love. It's easier to act your way into feeling something than it is to feel your way into acting. In other words, it's easier to simply choose to do some nice things for your customers — things they wouldn't normally expect you to do — than it is to wait until you feel like doing those nice things for your customers. Plus, once you start doing them, you'll probably find that you really enjoy your customers more than you thought.

Based on what we've just discussed, here are a few more thoughts for you to ponder about this driver called love.

1. **Make sure you love what you do.**

   Life's too short to waste it doing something you're not passionate about. If it's something you once were passionate about and think you can fall back in love again, then go for it. However, if you've never really loved what you're doing — or it's been so long and you don't think you'll ever get it back, then maybe it's time to create an exit plan — and that's okay! If you're the one holding your company back, it's best for everyone (you, your family, your customers, your potential customers, and your community) that you leave and find something that you're passionate about and willing to give 110% to once again. There's nothing wrong with starting all over again. In fact, it's the entrepreneurial way.

2. **If there's something in your work environment that's killing your love, then change your work environment.**

   One of the exercises that I regularly encourage my clients to do is to take out a piece of paper and draw a traffic light the length of the page on the left hand side of the paper (i.e a large vertical rectangle with three large circles in it — red, yellow, and green).

Then, next to the red light I ask them to write down all the things that they're currently doing that are draining energy away from them. Next to the yellow light I ask them to write down all the things that they're currently doing that they're indifferent to. And then, finally, I have them write down all the things that they're currently doing that energize them.

As you can probably guess, the list next to the red light is usually pretty long and extensive. The list next to the yellow light is moderate in size. And the list next to the green light is usually very small—and then they wonder why they're not very excited or passionate about the work they're doing. Hello! When most of what you do drains you, who would want to do more of that?

So what I encourage them to do is to take a look at the red light list and then determine which of those items will come off their list this month, then this quarter and then this year so that by the same time next year, the red light list is much smaller and the green light list much larger.

3. **Make sure you hire people you like (as well as take on clients you like).**

    Again, life's too short to surround ourselves with people we don't like to be around—people who take life away from us or who annoy us or whose personalities rubs us the wrong way.

    When you own this tactic, it makes everything else we've talked about in this book so much easier. For example, it's much easier to practice MBWA with people you like. It's much easier to coach and leverage people you like. It's much easier to encourage people you like. It's much easier to work on projects with people you like (than those you don't). And the more you like them and do the above practices with, the higher the love and morale quotient of your business will be—which, will ultimately translate into higher productivity, increased profits, and a lift off from your current plateau.

So if you want to break through your current plateau and get back on a double-digit growth curve, make sure you unleash the incredible power of this final driver: the love driver. It really can change everything!

While you may have started off this chapter thinking that love really isn't all that critical to building a bigger, better, faster and more profitable business (or organization), hopefully, you're ending it believing it is. Love really is critical if you want to break through a plateau and get back on a double-digit growth curve.

Well, there you have it. You now know the ten drivers of accelerated growth. All that's left is for you to implement them. So, make sure you answer the questions scattered throughout this book and then execute the ideas you need to implement.

Once you do — and your culture begins to change — everything else will change as well. "All of a sudden" all those ideas, tactics, and strategies that didn't seem to work before, will. And before you know it, you'll be back on a double-digit growth curve! Why? Because once you get the culture is right, everything else just falls into place!

To your accelerated success!

P.S. If you have any questions or comments, feel free to contact me by email at **bruce@WiredToGrow.com**

Applications for Driver #10: Love

1. On a scale or 1-10 (high) how would you rate your love for what you do?

2. On a scale or 1-10 (high) how would you rate your love for your employees?

3. On a scale or 1-10 (high) how would you rate your love for your customers?

4. Do you need to make any changes in how you work or what you do to make it easier for you to love what you do, as well as your employees and customers?

5. Do a traffic light analysis. Is there anything in your work environment that's killing your love for what you do? If so, what? And then, what can you do about it?

6. Evaluate your love factor for your staff. Is there anyone you have trouble loving? Why? Is there anything you can do to fix that?

7. What could you do this week to communicate your love for your people?

8. What are you major takeaways from this chapter?

9. What is one thing you can do this week to help you fall more in love with your work?

Summary Application of the 10 Drivers

1. On a scale of 1-10 (high) how would you rate each of the 10 drivers'
   impact on your organization (Note: this is a REVERSE ranking so a
   10 would mean that a driver has severely/negatively affected you.)

   1. Speed of implementation   1...2...3...4...5...6...7...8...9...10
   2. Leverage   1...2...3...4...5...6...7...8...9...10
   3. Optimization   1...2...3...4...5...6...7...8...9...10
   4. Focus   1...2...3...4...5...6...7...8...9...10
   5. Discipline   1...2...3...4...5...6...7...8...9...10
   6. Differentiation   1...2...3...4...5...6...7...8...9...10
   7. Addition   1...2...3...4...5...6...7...8...9...10
   8. Systems   1...2...3...4...5...6...7...8...9...10
   9. High Morale   1...2...3...4...5...6...7...8...9...10
   10. Love   1...2...3...4...5...6...7...8...9...10

2. Based on your scores, what do you think are the top three drivers
   that you're doing well/the best at (i.e. your lowest scores)?

3. What do you think you could you do over the next quarter to
   improve on those best performing drivers?

4. Again, based on your scores, what do you think are your three
   lowest performing drivers (i.e. your highest scores)?

5. If you were to pick one of those drivers to focus on over the next 90 days, which one do you think would have the greatest impact? Why?

6. For that top driver that you need to work on, list at least five ideas for how you could begin to turn that driver around?

7. If you were to pick one driver that you (personally) need to work on the most, which one would it be?

8. Based on everything you've read in this book, what do you think are the most important steps you need to take to help your business (or organization) break through its plateau?

9. With whom can you share what you learned (or were reminded of) from reading this book? When?

10. Finally, what is one action you can take with the next 24 hours as a response to what you've read in this book?

> "A good plan executed now is far preferable to a 'perfect' plan executed next week." Gen. Patton

Recommended Resource

How to Lead People Who Don't Think, Act and Feel Like You

If you've ever wrestled with leading people who just don't think, or act or feel like you, then you'll want to get your hands on this 5 CD/DVD course.

Most leaders make two classic mistakes. 1. They tend to lead everyone the same way and 2. The way they tend to lead is the way they like to be led.

Both of which are major mistakes — especially since most people aren't like them. In fact, no matter what your personality type, most of the people you'll ever lead in life won't be like you.

So, if you'd like to quickly know how to lead someone who isn't like you (from how they think to what the best kind of environment is for them to how to encourage them to how to best utilize them and so much more), you'll definitely want to go to

www.PersonalityTypeLeadership.com

Recommended Resource

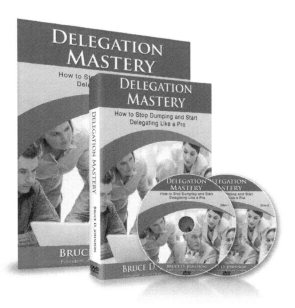

How to Stop Dumping and Start Delegating Like a Pro

If you're overwhelmed with way too much to do and not enough time in the day to get it all done, then you know, as we talked about in this book, that the key is to changing that is leveraging the time, talent, treasures, intellectual property, resources and networks of other people.

Unfortunately, most leaders aren't good leader. They're dumpers. They have a task that they want to get off their plates and they just dump that task off their plate into someone else's plate. Sound familiar?

What's worse, most leaders think that the problem is on the employee side. "If I just had some better employees ..." But the problem isn't primarily an employee problem, it's a leader problem. Dumping doesn't work.

So, if you'd like to turn that around so that you're a master delegator and your people are producing at an unbelievably high rate so that more is getting done with less on your plate, then go to

www.DelegationMastery.net

Ready to Build a Bigger, Better, Faster, And More Profitable Business?

Attention: Owner, Entrepreneur, or Service Professional

Would you like to ...

- Generate more revenue and profit?
- Attract and retain more customers?
- Gain an unfair advantage in your market space?
- Become a more effective leader?
- Raise your employees' productivity? And/or
- Create a more scalable and sustainable business that can consistently produce the kinds of results you want–whether you're there or not?

If so, then you'll want to contact us ASAP! Why? Because that's exactly what we do here at Wired to Grow.

We help owners, entrepreneurs and service professionals like you

- Generate strategies that can drive significant growth gains
- Create powerful direct marketing strategies that can rapidly accelerate your sales
- Develop compelling competitive advantages that differentiate you from everyone else in your market space
- Attract, retain, inspire and leverage a talented team of individuals toward a common cause
- Uncover new profit centers, often from untapped assets already in your business
- Build a loyal fan base of customers who want to buy more, more frequently, at higher price points
- Raise the level of execution excellence
- Design turnkey systems that make your business more predictable, sustainable, and enjoyable.
- And so much more …

Whether you're leading a $.5M, $1M, $5M, $10M, or $25M business, Wired to Grow can help you transform your business and take it to the next level--all while improving your bottom line profit and quality of life!

So, if you want to put your business on the fast track toward becoming the kind of business, organization or practice you've always dreamed of, make sure you contact us here at Wired To Grow as soon as possible!

Bruce D. Johnson, President
Wired To Grow

Phone: 301-602-0448
Fax: 240-536-9175

Website: www.WiredToGrow.com

About the Author

Bruce D. Johnson is a business growth strategist and leadership expert, as well as the President and Founder of Wired To Grow—a business growth coaching and consulting firm that helps owners, entrepreneurs and service professionals grow their businesses faster with less stress and more predictability.

Bruce is a passionate and dynamic communicator, as well as a content expert in small business growth issues—whether those issues are related to strategy, leadership, management, marketing or money.

In fact, it's one of the things that sets him apart from most consultants who tend to be single area content experts. Instead, Bruce brings a breadth of experience and insight to his clients and readers in all five key areas of executive attention—a breadth that you'll see demonstrated over and over again throughout this book.

Previous to starting Wired to Grow, Bruce spent twenty-two years in pastoral ministry, the last fifteen and a half of those at a church he started with just two families that grew to two thousand people and $2.7M in revenues his last year there.

Finally, at his core, Bruce is a family man. He and his wife, Jacquie, have been happily married for 27 years and have two adult-aged daughters, Chelsea and Brooke.

Note: If you're looking for a keynote speaker for your next event, and want to make it a home run, make sure you contact Bruce by emailing him at **bruce@WiredToGrow.com**. You can also see his current listing of message topics by going to www.WiredToGrow.com/speaking

Made in the USA
Charleston, SC
02 April 2012